Little Histories

SWEDES
FROM WHENCE THEY CAME

BY
JACK R. EVANS

Jack R. Evans
AKA J. Glenn Evans
14 JAN 2014

PUBLICATIONS
Seattle, Washington

FORWARD

The title of this book, *Swedes - From Whence They Came,* vividly describes the advent of repression, fire, pain and suffering that contributed to the moulding of the contemporary Swedish citizen.

The men and women, walking the busy streets of modern Stockholm, living in their high-rise flats and about in the land cannot easily contemplate the past tragic times that nearly decimated their ancestors by heinous criminal acts of selfish kings, religious zealots and their lackeys.

The progeny of those who suffered and died inherited not only their ancestor's strong physical attributes but also an admirable attitude of self-sufficiency, a love of freedom and of their fellowman.

In the contemporary country, the Swedish people still fish and log in those woods that protected the peasant from his high and mighty foe. Yet, Sweden, in the forefront with its auto industry, shows a genuine concern for the world environment by limiting auto production to reduce the impact of their factories' potential industrial pollution. This is only one example of the great advances over Sweden's long arduous history that show tremendous progress away from primitive times of fear, famine, war, pestilence and destruction.

Sweden moves forward, yet with its own unique and independent attitude. Still, she holds her hand out to the world. The committed and continuing benevolence of Citizen Nobel, who produced items of mass mayhem, echoes the dichotomy of those who sowed age-old destruction that annealed its citizens in a crucible of tragedy. They are now endowed with a strong and cohesive national character. The bad guys lost!

> William A. Murdoch
> Written as a true friend and
> admirer of Jack Evans in
> appreciation of his undying
> energy and creativity

(206)682-1268
LIBRARY OF CONGRESS CATALOG NO. 92-85013
ISBN 1-877882-05-4

DEDICATED

TO

THOMAS A. ALBERG

ACKNOWLEDGMENTS

Our special thanks to all who gave generously of their time and help in making this history possible. We deeply appreciate the help and encouragement of Thomas A Alberg of Alberg & Associates Inc; Marianne Forssblad of Nordic Heritage Museum; William A. Mordoch, Dr. Kay F. Reinartz, Ivar Stein of The Swedish Portrait Archives and the University of Stockholm who directed us to them; The Swedish Institute in Stockholm and Swedish Ambassador Anders Thunborg, Margareta Paul, Assistant to the Cultural Counselor for directing us to the Institute; the Seattle Swedish Consulate; those dedicated historians listed in our bibliography and to Rune Lindbom, my first Swedish friend, now deceased.

Many thanks to Bill and Sherry of Lubic & Lubic, Marilyn Holt of Into Print for desktop publishing, Don and Greg Swinford of Industrial Printers for printing and Mike Jaynes, for the cover design.

Picture on the front cover used courtesy of the Swedish Institute.

TABLE OF CONTENTS

Odin meant madness and was god of war,
who made men bold to face their enemy
Source: Swedish Institute

NEW SWEDEN

Few people realize that Sweden was the third of four
nations to establish a colony that became one of the
original thirteen American colonies. Nor do they
recognize the full extent of her contribution to the
development of the New World. Gustavus Adolphus
(Gustavus II) , king of Sweden, organized and
chartered a trading company in 1626 to colonize the
west shore of Delaware Bay. His objectives were to
develop Swedish communities in the New World that
would generate Swedish commerce and to spread the
Christian Gospel among the Indians. It was not until
the fall of 1637, five years after his death in battle, that
the Swedes first set sail for America from Gothenburg,
a city that Gustavus founded. The land which they
proposed to colonize had just been relinquished by
Charles I of England.

Peter Minuite was in command of two ships, *Key of
Kalmar*, a ship of war, and a smaller vessel called *Bird
Graffen*. The ships, loaded with crew and passengers,
were provisioned with ammunition and other
merchandise to be traded with the natives in the new
land.

The Swedes landed near what became Lews, Delaware
in the spring of 1638 and proceeded up the bay until
they reached the mouth of the Delaware River or where
Wilmington is presently located. A few acres of land
were purchased from an Indian chief and a small fort
was erected, which they called Fort Christina in honor
of their young queen. As new colonists arrived, the

Swedes purchased a larger tract of land from the Indians and called their colony New Sweden. Swedish relations with the Indians were always friendly as they bought land instead of taking it. Per Minuite was in command at Fort Christina until he died in 1640. Per Hollander then served as governor for almost two years before he returned to Sweden.

The Third Governor was Johan Printz . He weighed over 400 pounds, had piercing steel blue eyes, a prominent nose and a square jutting jaw. Printz took possession of the Island of Tinicum, located in the Delaware River about nine miles southwest of Philadelphia. This island became a part of Delaware, which was the first state to ratify the American Federal Constitution on December 7, 1787. Johan Printz built a brick residence on the island and a fort from which he governed New Sweden for the next ten years. When he returned home, Johan Printz became governor of the

Third Governor of New Sweden who colonized what later became Chester, Pennsylvania.
Source: Swedish Institute

Jonkoping Province in Sweden.

While in New Sweden, Printz and his Swedes colonized the area that was later to become Chester, Pennsylvania. Thus, the first European settlers in Pennsylvania were the Swedes, who were there to greet William Penn almost 50 years later.

Sweden's dream of a new world died after only 17 years. The Swedish capture of a nearby Dutch fort brought reprisal from the energetic Peter Stuyvesant, governor of the New Netherlands. This led to the Swedish governor's surrender to the Dutch in 1655. The Swedes stayed, but were under Dutch rule for the next nine years. Then, the English conquered the Dutch. With New Sweden under foreign domination, few Swedes emigrated to America for the next 200 hundred years.

OLD SWEDEN FROM WHENCE THEY CAME

Icelandic literature referred to Sweden as Svithiod. The Russian monk and chronicler, Nestor (1056-1114), referred to it as Rus. Sweden is located in Northern

Swedish flag first used during reign of
Gustavus Vasa 1523 – 1560
Source: Swedish Institute

Europe at the eastern and southernmost part of the Scandinavian peninsula and includes the Baltic islands of Oland and Gotland. The land area is about a 1,000 miles (1,610 kilometers) long and 250 miles (400 kilometers) wide. Sweden's 173,655 square miles include inland waters. Her boundry length, estimated at 6,100, includes 4,720 coastal miles. Stockholm is the capital. The Swedish flag is a three-pronged blue and yellow banner, which was first used during the reign of Gustavus Vasa (Gustavus I). The oldest Swedish flags known to exist are at Rijkmusemum, Armsterdam. They were captured by Dutch ships at Oresund in 1658.

Sweden's highest mountains lie along the Norwegian border. The terrain between the Caledonian Mountains and the Baltic Sea is mainly granite. Plains cover more than half of the region. Sweden's topography was formed by the Ice Ages. The Gulf of Bothnia freezes in the winter, but Stockholm's port is usually open.

Ice covered Sweden during the Ice Age. The great thaw began in Skane (Scania) about 12,000 years before Christ. The thaw was still proceeding in central Sweden 3,000 years later, or 9000 B.C. As the ice disappeared from southern Sweden, the willow, the dwarf birch, the reindeer and polar fox made their appearance. Then the hunters and fishermen, still at the flint and stone implement stage, came in search of food and land. First traces indicate human occupation about 6000 B.C., but first movement of people into Sweden probably occurred at the close of the glacial epoch - 12,000 B.C. Around Lake Ringsjon in Skane and at Sandarna there was human life at the extreme northwest and north coast of Scandinavia during most of the glaciation period. Some tracks of land apparently remained free of ice, even when the weather was in its coldest stages. Warming of the Atlantic waters brought moisture and a milder climate. The first Swedish settlements were primitive and life was an excruciating struggle for existence. Tribes of reindeer hunters roamed across the land bridge joining Sweden to the continent.

Agriculture came to Sweden by way of Denmark. Around 2500 B.C. the tribes seem to have acquired the rudiments of the cultivation of grain and the raising of livestock, mostly cattle and pigs. Peasant culture flourished in what became the provinces of Skane-Haland, Bohuslan and Vastergotland. The Boat-Ax culture of Europe arrived about 2000 B.C. Trade developed between the Roman empire and the Scandinavians.

Animal life in this northern land includes mountain hare, shrews, ermine, weasel, red squirrel, fox, badger, otter, mink, bear, wolf, lynx and elk. Elk are common to the entire area and are the most valuable game animal. The badger and otter are hunted for their skins, along with the thriving wild descendants of escaped mink. Bear and wolf are now protected as well as the lynx. Wild reindeer are now extinct, but domesticated herds remain in Lappland. Bird life consists of teal, snipe, golden plover, wagtail and waterfoul of the lakes. Birds of prey such as the golden eagle and the buzzard and the owl are to be found here. Few reptiles are in Sweden, but they do have the viper, which is their only poisonous snake. The rivers contain salmon, trout, char, pike, perch and sprat.

Physiognomy of the Swedish people is basically Nordic and characterized by a long slim body, oval face, blond hair and blue eyes. In Dalarna there is a different strain of uncertain prehistorical origin, who have heavy short bodies. Language is derived from the Nordic Viking age, and is similar to Danish and Norwegian.

Villages were plagued by three evils—war, crop failure and disease. There were long periods of relief from these factors, when great prosperity was enjoyed. The unwritten law of mutual aid and assistance was a vital factor in village communities. People followed the natural rule which was that you help me today and I will help you tomorrow. When tragedy such as sickness or accident struck a villager and a man could not sow his field or gather in his hay, his neighbors helped him without compensation. All they asked was that he be there when they needed help. Work done where payment was required was usually paid for by return of work or other farm commodities. In this helpful society a neighbor was not taken advantage of for profit.

When there was an important task requiring many workers, they pulled together and afterwards enjoyed a feast and merrymaking. An old Swedish proverb said, "with both hand and mouth we can lend each other a helping hand." This meant work with camaraderie. The hay-feast usually ended in July and was one of the biggest events every year. Village haying had to be completed by St. Olof's Day or the 29th of July. The evening feast was held on the last day of July with festivities including dances, games in the barn or on the rock ledges. It lasted all night and after sunup the weary celebrators took to bed. The hay-feast has now long vanished, but is remembered in literature.

Flax, which reached Scandinavia about the Bronze Age, brought a revolution in clothing. Prior to its entry skins and the fur of beasts of prey provided clothing. Later it was hides of domestic cattle and sheep. Flax was one of the earliest plants to be cultivated in the world and was domesticated before 2000 B.C. Seeds over 4,000 years old were found in the the Egyptian tombs. Flax processing involved the whole village and called for a work- feast. There were reaping, bleaching, spinning and sewing to be done.

CONTACTS WITH THE ANCIENTS

About 300 B.C. the Greek sailor, Tytheas, visited the northland. He described the land that became Sweden. "The sun rose almost as soon as it set and the night would last almost a half a year. There were fen-lands and islands. The ocean brought costly amber to this fabulous island country."

Sweden was visited by the Romans at the time of Emperor Augustus Caesar . The Romans were attracted to the area because of the amber and a trade in this item of luxury developed. Pliny the Elder wrote of Scandinavia and the islands of the northern ocean. Tacitus described a tribe of Suiones:

> The people respected wealth, were obedient
> and one man ruled supreme, unchallenged.
> They maintained arms and powerful fleets.
> Their ships had a prow at each end, with a peak
> to be driven forwards or backwards.

These boats probably came into use prior to the third century before Christ. Samples have been excavated at Hjortspring in Denmark.

About 150 A.D. Ptolemy, the Egyptian astrologer and geographer from Alexandria, drew a map of the countries on the Baltic Sea. He called Sweden Scandia and on his maps it appeared as the largest and most easterly of the four islands in the Germanic Ocean. Peoples of the Mediterranean had little contact with this northern country until 50 years prior to the birth of Christ. Roman contact with Scandinavia came by trade routes along the rivers. Glass goblets and bronze vessels made in the Roman Empire as well as Roman silver coins have been found on Swedish soil.

During the sixth century contact with Europe brought trade in costly skins and precious metals. The foremost tribes were the Svear and the Gotlanders. Swedish life in the sixth century was in rural village communities. Communal labor was used for greater safety, which benefited cattle-raising and agriculture. This expanding period of farming and maritime exploits established the base for the Viking campaigns of the ninth and tenth centuries. These campaigns provided the entry of Swedish tribes into history as merchants and pirates outside the Baltic Sea. Wealth first started to come to Sweden from plundering the disintegating Roman Empire during the fifth and early sixth century.

Ancient Arabian coins found in Sweden testify also to an active trade with Arabia. Ibn Fadhlan in the tenth century wrote that he had never seen more statelier men. They were as tall as palm trees, ruddy cheeked and red haired. He indicated that each man carried an ax, knife and sword, and were not caught without these weapons. Even earlier the Arabian writer, Ibn Dustah, wrote that the Swedish Vikings' sole operation was trade in sable, squirrel and other skins. They were brave and valiant. When they came up against a people, they utterly plundered, vanquished or made slaves of them. They did not display any horsemanship, as all of their warlike activities were performed from ships.

VIKING PERIOD

During the Swedish Viking period from 800 to 1050 A.D. the main social order was kin. Family honor was defended. During this period three individual Scandinavian kingdoms developed, namely Norway, Denmark and Sweden. It was a period of great plundering and extensive trading expeditions with slaves as the main commodity.

The Swedish Vikings sailed across the Baltic and conducted raids against the Slavs. These Swedes were called Rus or Ros by the Slavs because they came from Roslagen on the Swedish side of the Baltic. It was from these adventuresome Rus or Swedish Vikings, who had settled and ruled the lands across the Baltic, that the name Rusland and later Russian is derived. In 862 a Rus or Scandinavian named Rurik was made king at Novgorod. His descendants sat on the Russian throne until Boris Godunov came to power in 1598.

Chronicles from the Russian monk, Nestor (1056-1114), reveal how the Swedes brought law and order into Russia. Larger towns were placed under the control of powerful Swedish representatives who obtained trading advantages. Conquered towns were often situated in key positions along rivers and lakes. Vikings' ships were constructed so that they could be dragged on rollers between lakes and navigable rivers. Nestor further noted that the Vikings could load and unload cargos under the most adverse circumstances in the most difficult landing places.

Swedes — From Whence They Came

The Swedes in Russia of the ninth century were too few in number to remain the dominant race, so they became submerged in the immense Slavic mass.

SWEDES AND THEIR FORESTS

Forests have always provided Sweden's main defense. An enemy's progress could be hindered by trees cut across roads and trails. The fallen trees also served as forts. In the woods the natives had the advantage while foreign legionaires often lost their way. Peasants would use guerrilla tactics before the word became known. They would strike as it pleased them, hide when not fighting, regroup and attack again. German legionaires, called in by Swedish kings to fight against their own rebellious peasants, were almost useless in the deep forest. They were terrified of every bush. Behind each one there might be a man with a crossbow. The term guerrilla warfare was first used during the Spanish revolt against Napoleon. It has since been used to describe resistance or freedom movements anyplace in the world.

Many Swedes owed their lives to the forest. Food and refuge from foreign armies and their own government were to be found in the forest. From tree-bark, they could make their daily bread. They found meat from game and materials for dwelling construction in the forests. Lakes and rivers contained plentiful fish. Often there were farm animals to steal from other peasants whose farms were near the edge of the forest. There were wild berries in season. Tools and utensils were made of wood. Their boats, their spinning wheels, their cart wheels and clogs for footwear were made of wood.

The forest served the needs of individuals who wanted freedom from the community. It was escape from established customs, rules and laws. Ancient court rulings had a term which meant, "gone to the forest." People who sought voluntary exile were called Skogsman, meaning woodsmen. Since adultery was punishable by death, many lovers sought refuge in the forests. Woodsmens' dwellings were often no more than a hole dug in the ground or tents made from tree branches. The tall tales of trolls and giants first came from these forest people.

With the development of a class society the freedoms common to the Swedish peasants during the early Middle Ages were greatly reduced. Limitations imposed by the upper classes left little opportunity for deviation. Peasants were not alone in seeking forest refuge. Members of powerful clans often fled to the forest for political reasons. Unfortunately, with world population growth and diminishing forests, this freedom to "go to the forest" has been greatly reduced. With modern societies having no forest refuge, the individual is often at the mercy of the state, an institution that was originated to protect the rights of the individual, but which often has become the tool of the few.

PEASANTS AND POVERTY

Peasants, small landowners and laborers on the Swedish, Danish and Norwegian borders were often related or were friends and neighbors. These border provinces are known today as Vastergotland, Smaland, Halland, Skane and Blekinge. On both sides of the border, from the peasants' point of view, their national leaders did nothing for them, only to them. From their own governments, the peasants sought only to be left alone and in peace. Opposing government forces would encroach from their side, cross the border, plunder, rape and destroy. The peasants of these border communities often made independent treaties with their peasant neighbors on the other side. Each would forewarn his neighbor across the border of impending raids from their own national government. They would agree not to cross the border and participate in such raids. This attitude of the border peasants was well illustrated in the war between Norway and Sweden. Two peasants met at the border with guns in hand, ready to kill. The Norwegian threw down his weapon and said something to the effect of "Well! If it isn't Ola from Kattbo!" Ola also threw down his weapon and the two fell into each other's arms with enthusiastic greetings. These peasant treaties across the borders survived for many generations until Gustavus Vasa (Gustavus I) put an end to them by imposing severe penalties.

Over the centuries Sweden has suffered many droughts and floods, which often brought on famine. A Swede has been described as one who has the ability to display a free spirit in the face of misery and poverty. To overcome poverty some would pack up their belongings and seek another patron or farm to work on. Others would head for America to escape the poverty. Whole families would leave everything behind and head for an unknown fate in the new world.

The famine years of 1596 to 1598 devastated whole populations with starvation, disease and death. A delayed flood after the spring planting in 1596 ruined the seed. Day after day, the rains fell. Clothes rotted on people's backs; hay molded and rotted in the barns. Cattle, made sick by the ruined fodder, died by the hundreds. The wetness continued through the summer and fall and by then the reserves of previous harvests were gone. People ate leaves of hazel bushes, buds, hay, straw and roots. They made flour out tree bark and pulverized bones. Weakened, they hardly had the strength to grind the bark into flour. Many starved to death that winter and the following spring. Gallows were strung with corpses of those who had dared to steal anything eatable. Bark bread, when available, was the daily fare. Two more years of crop failures followed, but were less severe.

Certain taxes were remitted as there was nothing else to take. The royal bailiffs, when they could collect, often kept the levy for themselves. Poor folks, who attended church, were told that this was God's punishment for their sinful lives.

People observed what their animals ate and they would eat the same. They noted that elk, deer and rabbits nibbled bark from deciduous trees. Horses ate spruce and aspen bark as well as leaves. Many animals can digest cellulous, but not man.

One Swede described his family's poverty and manners, which were like most other families at that time:

His mother prepared the food in the kitchen, and when it was time to eat the men took up the whole table, leaving her no room to sit down. When they finished, if there was anything left, she would approach and eat the leftovers. Often she would stand at the stove and be content with a few boiled potatoes. There was rarely room at the table for women, who slinked on the sidelines like dogs to be contented with a bone.

SWEDISH CUSTOMS

Almost to the extent of self-effacement, the Swedes are taught from early childhood to always be modest. Tell a Swedish lady she has a nice dress, and she might say, "Oh! This old rag."

With Swedes, it takes time to get acquainted. They like to move in the same circle of friends; it helps to have a letter of recommendation. Once you break the barrier, you have a true and sincere friend. Crack the shell of reserve and you will find warmth and goodwill.

The Swedes do not have many legal problems. They are a law- abiding people whose lives are ruled by conformity and compliance. A handshake will often conclude a deal. They will trust their fellowman until the other proves himself unworthy. They can be as stubborn as mules, when it comes to standing up for their principles.

They have a natural urge to do first-class work with attention to the smallest detail. A contankerous nature is revealed to the one who will compromise on job quality.

The word, skal, initially meant a bowl or vessel. In ancient times a host may have greeted his guest with, "Ta for er ur skalen," which translates to help yourselves from the bowl. Each person dipped his scoop into a bowl. Over the years this was reduced down to "Skal" which became a symbol of hospitality.

Feast celebrations take time. A celebration commemorating an outgoing alderman might last as long as ten to twelve days.

Village folkways dated from ancient times and often provided a harsh community rule. To marry outside one's own village was usually forbidden. This changed when society became aware of the dangers of inbreeding. Violators of village law were usually punished by fines which went into the community entertainment account. Lady Justice showed a fair hand as the lawbreakers could participate in the feast for which their fines helped to finance.

The villages often had community assistance programs. When a young couple married, a collection was taken to help them set up their household. This was known in Sweden as the bethrothal round. The girl went from house to house and she would be given wool, flax and hemp. Her fiance went from farm to farm with a sack. At each farm he was given half-peck of grain with which to sow his field for the first time. A woman in childbirth received special attention from the other women, who would bring to her tasty porridge and butter.

The territory of each village was confined to perhaps a half a dozen miles. People of other parishes were considered foreigners and were regarded with suspicion.

Village life was moralistic. Punishment for fornication was harsh and adultery could bring death, plus the clergy held eternal damnation over their heads.

Unmarried couples were not permitted in public to hold hands or go about arm-in-arm. In ancient times for relief of their passions young couples could participate in what was called "bundling." With both of their parents' knowledge and permission, a boy could visit a girl, spend the night in her bed with both of them fully dressed. They were not permitted sex, but no limits were set on their caresses. If by chance the laws of nature prevailed and temptation overpowered them and the girl did become pregnant, a crossbow wedding solved the problem. The Lutheran Church spoiled this native fun by condemning the practice of bundling as sinful. Nevertheless, the custom was popular and continued until attitudes liberalized and boys and girls could associate in public. Dating from ancient heathen days, the peasant moral code was suspended once each year on the shortest midsummer night. To pacify the God of fertility, sex was permitted to the unwed on that night.

SWEDISH FOODS

One of the earliest known Swedish cookbooks was published anonymously in 1650. The title was "Een Lijten Kockebook" or small cookbook. A modern version of this book, edited by Per Erik Wahlund, was published in 1962. It is called "En Gammal Svensk Kokbok," which means an old Swedish cookbook.

The smorgasbord came from Sweden, that savory festival of food consisting of hot and cold meats, smoked and pickled fish, cheeses, sausages, salads and bread and butter and sometimes schnapps (liquor).

Coffee

A Swede loves his coffee. He was exposed to this delightful brew after a visit to Turkey in 1657 by the Swedish Ambassador.

Bags of coffee beans arrived at Goteborg in 1685. There were not many buyers as no one knew how to use the new product. Forty- three years later in 1728 there were over 15 coffee houses in Stockholm. First coffee customers were probably traveling merchants, sailors, or soldiers of fortune. Coffee became a great favorite of the poets and troubadours before it finally reached the average Swedish home.

In 1817 a notice posted in Skane prohibited parishioners from partaking of uddeballare, a form of spiked coffee. A later law forbidding the use of any coffee was abolished in 1822 and the Swedes have been coffee enthusiasts since.

Bread

An old Swedish proverb states, "Unhappy beyond all others is the brodless." Brod is the Swedish word for bread, which comes from a 12th century adaptation of the German word, "brot."

Swedish peasants produced four types of grain - barley, rye, wheat and oats. Rye and oats came first. Wheat, which had first come to Sweden many ages later, is first mentioned as being imported into Iceland in *Egil's Saga*, whose hero was the Icelandic poet and adventurer, Egill Skallagrimsson (910-990), which was believed to have been written in 1220 by Snorri Sturluson, the famous Icelandic historian. Wheat was limited to the diet of the upper classes in the early Middle Ages. This food of the gentry was limited to festive occasions for others. Wheat bread was utilized in weddings, christenings, funerals and other church activities. Wheat bread did not come into general use until after Christianity's triumph in Scandinavia. It was not until the 20th century that white bread became a regular part of the Swedish diet.

During the Middle Ages there were several types of bread baked in Sweden. In the southern and eastern parts of Sweden it was fermented and leavened rye bread. In western and northern Sweden a flat thin bread was produced. Olaus Magnus, in his *History of the Nordic Peoples*, tells of farms in Vastergotland where women baked rye bread as large as warrior shields. Magnus also told of a different type of bread that would remain fresh and eatable for twenty years, but there were many rules that had to be observed in its baking and storing.

Bark Bread

Sweden, populated by farmers, was often left helpless by the forces of nature such as crop failures, drought and floods. Early autumn frosts also ruined crops. People of a province, whose crops failed, simply starved. Roads between provinces were sparse or non-existent and made the transport of help often impossible. During famine years the peasant could only turn to the forest for his bread.

Tree bark used in the making of this bread came from the layer located right under the rough outer bark. This was scaled off with a scraper, hung in the open air to dry, then beaten or crushed and ground into flour. Pine was the most available tree, but three deciduous trees, elm, aspen and silver birch, yielded the most bark. Elm was the favorite. Bark bread was still quite common a 100 years ago in the countryside when there was a crop failure. The bark used contained cane sugar or a substance similar to grape sugar as well as protein and minerals. The taste was a little sour to the tongue, but otherwise it was tasteless. This food kept many Swedes from starving during famine periods.

Other famine bread was made of of chopped husks and straw, which were ground and mixed with flour or corn meal. This concoction was difficult to eat. It was hard to swallow and it took a mouthful of water to get each bite down. Reindeer moss was also utilized. People gathered hazel and heather buds, which were ground and kneaded into dough. Cornmeal or flour would be added if available to make it more palatable. Eaten over long periods of time, bark bread was harmful to the stomach and caused sickness. Such desperate times were probably last seen during the hard years of 1860, when Sweden had its last great famine period.

Cheese and Butter Making

Men were forbidden to participate in the cheese or butter making process. This was woman's work in Sweden. Sweden's last Catholic archbishop had written during the middle of the 16th century that as a small child he had helped his mother carry milk. He was only permitted to go to the threshold of the house where cheese was being made. A man's presence was thought to influence the curdling of the milk by spoiling its coagulation. Women also believed that if a man were to come into the house where a woman was churning butter, no butter would appear until he had gone.

The women of Vastergotland may have been the early cheese makers, but it took two strong men to carry their gigantic cheeses and that was with difficulty. Of the major cheese producing countries Sweden ranked twelfth in 1954, producing 122 million pounds or 2.4 percent, somewhat below production in Greece, but slightly more than Switzerland. The United States was the major producer with 1,354 million pounds.

CITIES AND CASTLES

Uppsala

Uppsala Castle, started in 1548 by Gustavus Vasa, was still unfinished at the reign of his great-granddaughter, Christina. That part which had been readied for occupancy gave Christina the spacious and elegant apartments that enabled her to have the large assemblies she so relished.

Uppsala Castle today with construction
started by Gustavus Vasa 1548
Source: Swedish Institute

Gothenburg or Goteborg

An omen created this city, which was founded by Gustavus Adolphus in 1619. The young monarch of 25, ruler of Sweden for the past eight years, was a strong believer in omens. During a visit to the broad estuary of the Gota River a small bird landed at his feet, seeking refuge from an eagle. To him this was a good omen. He ordered that a city be built here and fortified against the Danes. This was Sweden's second outlet into the Kattegat, that broad arm of the North Sea, which was their only access to commerce with Western Europe.

Swedes — From Whence They Came

Dutch ways were highly esteemed by Gustavus Adolphus. Just as Peter the Great of Russia would do in a later time, Gustavus Adolphus imported Dutch planners and builders to create his new city and to help develop Swedish commerce and industry. Since the Dutch could not conceive a city without canals, Gothenburg has canals as well as streets.

Gothenburg first began trading with the British East Indies about 1730. Later, it prospered from the Napoleonic Wars. With Napoleon's ban on English trade, British merchandise was shipped here, re-labeled, declared of Swedish origin and reshipped to other ports. At one time in 1810, there were as many as 1,124 merchant vessels lying just outside Gothenburg harbor, waiting to be processed. This trade ceased with the fall of Napoleon. Over 300 Gothenburg firms went bankrupt within two years after Waterloo. Business at this port remained stagnant for the next several decades.

Skokloster

Skokloster estate was once a Cistercian Convent. Gustavus Vasa confiscated it, doing essentially what his contemporary, Henry VIII, was doing to the Catholics in England. This castle was later awarded by Gustavus Adolphus to his field marshal, Hermann von Rangel.

Karlstad

Norway wanted her own king and complete independence. It was at Karlstad, 60 miles from the Norwegian border, that the Union of Norway and Sweden was dissolved in 1905. The leader of the Norwegian movement was the great nationalist and poet, Bjornstjerne Bjornson. King Osker VII of Sweden summoned the Riksdad, which voted to dissolve the union if Norway would agree to certain terms. Delegates from both nations met at Karlstad and after long negotiations came to an agreement of dissolution. Norway would discontinue the fortifications, which they had begun along the Swedish border. There would be a neutral no-man's-land on both sides of the line in which no military preparations could be undertaken. Both would submit future disputes to the Hague Court of International Arbitration.

Karlstad today is a busy industrial-commercial town, whose main business is timber, wood pulp, and machinery for making wood pulp and paper products.

Vittskovle

One of the grandest old places in Skane is Vittskovle Castle, which was built in 1550 by the Brahes family. There are more than 100 rooms with secret passageways and the castle is completely surrounded by a moat.

Skane

This southern Swedish province is comprised of
Kristianstad and Malmohus counties. Land area is
4,356 miles and the population in 1970 was slightly
under a million people. Just to the north of Skane is
Smaland, sometimes described as having fields which
bear more stones than crops.

KINGS AND QUEENS OF SWEDEN

Olof Skotkonung
(Family ruled 995-1060)

One of the first Swedish monarchs that history records is Olaf Skottkonung, descendant of a King Eric of Uppsala. He and his sons ruled Sweden from 995 to 1060. This was the period in which the frontiers between Norway, Sweden and Denmark were formally drawn.

Eric IX
(King 1150-1160)

Eric IX, known as Saint Eric, is considered the patron saint of the Swedes. Eric led a crusade into Finland in 1157 and the defeated Finns were forced to be baptized. His grandson, Eric Cnutsson or Eric X, ruled as king from 1208 to 1216.

Birger Magnusson (Birger II), grandson of Birger Jarl, held court in the 1300's at Stegeborg, an island castle used as a stronghold against other Skandinavian Vikings. His father, Magnus I, divided his kingdom among three sons.

Birger II
(King 1290-1318)
(Under regency 1290-1302)
(1280-1321)

King Birger's two younger brothers visited him at one of the castles near Sigpuna, captured and imprisoned him and his family for over two years. When released, Birger's status was no better than that of his younger brothers. His revenge came at Yuletide in 1317. During this festive season Birger invited his younger brothers to visit him at Nykoping Castle. He put them in chains and placed them in one of his foulest dungeons. When the brothers' followers attempted rescue in 1318, they found the princes dead. So enraged were they that King Birger had to flee to Denmark. In his haste to depart Birger left behind his young son, Magnus. When the king could not be found, they put young Magnus to death. News of his son's fate hastened the death of King Birger.

Den Store Fursten Birger Jarlg afbild, befkådad, s= Rawagtelig Slätt, uti Finland år 1940, Sedan han dripit Finnar, odi tavoagtaner, till Den Efkrifteliga tron, odi Ättes Efter lade Gründen till Stoeckholm .

Birger Jarl – Grandfather of Birger II
Source: The National Swedish Art Museums Swedish Portrait Archives

Magnus II (Magnus Eriksson)
(King 1319-1365)
(Under regency 1319-1332)
(1316-1374)

On Mora Plain of Dalecarlia leaders from all the provinces gathered to choose a new king. Their choice was the three year old son of Eric, oldest of King

Birger's brothers, who had perished in his dungeon.
This child king, also named Magnus like King Birger's
son who had been killed, was known as Magnus
Ericsson. He was also heir through his mother to the
throne of Norway.

Being only three years old, he ruled under a regent
from 1319 to 1332. Most of his life was spent in
Sweden, where he tried to control the nobility. He was
dethroned at the age of 47 in 1363 by the Royal
Council of Swedes. He retired to Norway where he
drowned in 1374.

Eric XIII
(King 1412-1439)
(1382-1459)

King Eric XIII of Sweden, from Pomerania, was also
King Eric VII of Denmark. He was the sole ruler under
the Union of Kalmar (1397-1412). Affairs of the realm
were controlled by his grandaunt, Margaret. During a

Stegeborg Castle was an island castle used as defense against
other Scandinavian Vikings
Source: The National Swedish Art Museums
Swedish Portrait Archives

period of great dissension he was driven out of Sweden by the uprising of the Dalecarlians (1434- 1436). After he lost his Danish crown in 1439 Eric fled to Gotland, an island in the Baltic Sea off the coast of Sweden, where he lived out the rest of his days as a pirate.

Charles VIII (Karl)
(King 1448-1457, 1464-1465, and 1467-1470)
(1408-1470)

Karl Knutsson Bonde was an on again-off again king. He served as Sweden's head of state three separate times and also as king of Norway from 1449 to 1450. This was a world record. Ericus Olia, a chronicler and contemporary of Karl VIII, described him as an often timid intriguer who could be downright cowardly. He was considered patriotic to the extent of helping to create and maintain a free and independent Swedish Kingdom, but to his own rebellious subjects he had no scruples about being ruthless. His ambition was to expand the monarchy over both the nobility and the church as well as the commoners. Karl Knutsson with his stately appearance truly looked and acted like a king. He was considered the leader of the Swedes, but was twice repulsed by the freedom-loving common people.

Karl Knutsson Bonde (Karl VIII) came from one of Sweden's oldest aristocratic families. His linage is traced back to Saint Eric. He was a well-traveled, brilliant and educated nobleman. He could be generous to friends and supporters, but vicious to dissenters. Perntnoke's sculpture at Gripsholm Castle depicts him as a magnificent, stately knight. Perntnoke also created the famous sculpture of "Saint George and the Dragon" located in Stockholm Cathedral.

Karl Knutsson left his family estate in the Smaland district and joined forces with Engelbrekt, the peasant rebel. Bonde's contribution towards liberation was small from a military standpoint. In power after Engelbrekt's death he was ruthless in crushing peasant revolts.

Karl Knutsson Bonde only Swedish King to rule three different times and over thrown twice
Source: The National Swedish Art Museums

In 1441 when King Eric XIII (Erik) lost his Swedish crown, Karl Knutsson Bonde reached for it while still earl marshal, but was unsuccessful. The Swedish crown fell to Kristoffer of Bavaria. Karl Knutsson Bonde had to be satisfied with the province of Finland as a fief. When the king appeared together with the earl marshal, the short, squatty form of Kristoffer was underscored by Karl's regal stature. Furthermore, on Kristoffer's assumption of power the weather turned dreadful. There followed a terrible famine and the peasants blamed the king for the weather. Kristoffer fell into great disfavor with the commoners, who called him the "Bark King." He was reported to be a gambler and whoremaster, who spent most of his time drinking. Modern research has shed a better light on this unfortunate king. Kristoffer had made important judiciary reforms, and most important of all, he had never burned an insubordinate peasant as kingly Karl was to do.

Sweden was an electoral monarchy in the mid 1400's with the king being elected by the nobility. At the death of King Kristoffer in 1448, Karl Knutsson Bonde received 63 votes for king and his two opponents, Bengt and Mils, received only eight votes between them. The country had been experiencing the severe "Kristoffer" drought. A downpour occurred the day that Karl Knutsson arrived in Stockholm as one of the prospects for the crown. To the peasants it was an omen that God was well pleased with Karl Knutsson Bonde.

Now, at last, the Swedes had a "Swedish" king, Karl VIII, as Karl Knutsson was to be known. His first reign lasted until 1457. Starting with his first year as king in 1448, his popularity continued to decline with each passing year. After the 9th year, the peasants had enough of their Swedish king and those in Uppland revolted. King Karl VIII (Karl Knutsson) was overthrown. This revolt was led by Jons Bengtsson Oxenstierna, archbishop of Sweden. This highly educated man had been the Rector of Leipzig University. He was also a soldier, who could wield the sword and lance as well as the Word. Karl Knutsson's policies towards the church and the nobles' estates had turned away the archbishop, who had been an earlier supporter. The peasants, fleeced and extorted by taxes, also clamored for a new king. It mattered little to the peasants whether the king was a Dane or a Swede, as long as their burdens were relieved.

Archbishop Jons Bengtsson, in taking up arms against King Karl VIII, removed his pontificals and bishop's miter and declared that he would don them no more until the problems had been corrected. During a snow storm the archbishop put on armor and led a troop of knights into battle against the king on the ice of Lake Malaren. Victory was his; Karl Knutsson fled to Danzig, where he remained in comfort for the next seven years. This Swedish king had absconded with a great fortune that had been extorted in the form of taxes from his Swedish subjects.

After nine years of a Swedish king, Karl VIII, the Swedes decided that the Danes were not so bad. Christian I of Oldenburg was proclaimed king of Sweden at Mora Stones in Uppland on July 2, 1457. The Swedish nobles found it most agreeable to have a king who lived in Denmark. He was out of sight and they could do pretty well as they pleased. The church, too, had grown rich and powerful and liked having a Danish king who left them alone.

Bonde's successor did not fare well either. Christian I was constantly in financial straits and became known by the nickname, "Christian Bottomless Empty Pocket." As in an old Swedish saying, Christian "lied the sack full."

After six years of Christian's Danish rule, the peasants of Uppland rebelled again. After they occupied part of Stockholm, an armistice was called. Again, they found that the king was not to be trusted. Christian did not honor his word and there was another peasant bloodbath. Almost 1,000 men were slaughtered on August 21, 1463. Even those who sought sanctuary in a monastery were killed by Christian's men. Archbishop Oxenstierna, who had originally called for a Union of Kalmar king and had favored Christian over Bonde, now opposed him. The archbishop was carted off to Denmark and thrown into prison. This helped to bring on a general Swedish uprising, with Bishop Kettil Karlsson Vasa of Linkoping also taking up arms. Christian I was defeated the next year by the peasant army in the Battle of Haraker in 1464. During this battle Sten Gustavsson Sture, a young nephew of Karl Knutsson Bonde, showed outstanding courage and presence of mind. Some years later he would become ruler of Sweden and after his death would be known as Sten Sture the Elder.

After six years of rule by Christian I, Karl Knutsson Bonde's misdeeds paled. He was called back from exile and made king a second time. This peasant group, which recalled Knutsson in 1464, was believed to be the first Swedish parliament.

Karl VIII (Karl Knutsson) ruled only five months this second time, the shortest reign in Swedish history. His old enemy, Archbishop Oxenstierna, had been released from Danish prison. The archbishop had come home and joined forces with Kettil Karlsson Vasa. They made it so difficult for King Karl that he abdicated a second time and made an undertaking this time that he would never attempt to be king again. In settlement King Karl received the Finnish provinces of Raseborg and Korsholm as a fief and was allowed retain his royal title.

The government in the next two years was in a state of confusion. Kettil Karlsson Vasa seized power, but by August of 1465 Jons Bengtsson Oxenstierna took over. He in turn was succeeded by Erik Axelsson Tott. Oxenstierna had the support of the Union party and the friendship of the Danes, but was opposed by the well-matched Totts. Victory ultimately went to a third party, which again recalled Karl Knutsson Bonde from his Finnish exile and made him king again in November of 1467 in spite of his promise not to seek the kingship position again.

Archbishop Oxenstierna made another attempt to overthrow Karl Knuttson, but failed. There had been five regimes in a period of three years. Karl maintained his throne this time until his death at age 62, which came on May 15 of 1470. Out of the 22 years between 1448 and 1470, Bonde had ruled for only 12 years.

Sten Sture the Elder
(Regent 1470-1503)
(1440?-1503)

Sten Sture, to be known after his death as Sten Sture the Elder, was the first of the Stures to rule. He was Karl Knutsson Bonde's nephew; his mother was Bonde's half sister. Sture's full name was Sten Gustavsson Sture. Sten always identified himself as regent rather than king, even though he exercised full kingship power. He had seen too many nobles struggle and kill to become king. Being known only as regent might be some protection against envy of the other aristocrats.

Sten Sture came to power in 1470. It was said that 5,000 pints of good strong German beer helped to bring about his election at Arboga. For the next 50 years, the the Stures dominated Swedish politics. Sten still had to contend with Christian I, the Union of Kalmar king from Denmark. He consolidated his power by defeating Christian in the Battle of Brunkeberg just outside of Stockholm on October 10, 1471.

The wooden sculpture of Saint George and the Dragon commemorates that victory at Brunkeberg, which took place on Saint George's Day. The statue is to be found in Storkyrkan or Stockholm Cathederal. This church, built in 1264, is where Swedish kings are crowned. The sculptor was the German artist, Bernt Notke. It is said that Sten Sture the Elder, himself, stood model for this work and donated it to the church. The dragon, whom he is slaying, represents King Christian I.

Sten Sture the Elder was an anomaly for his times. He did not kill his enemies nor were peasants burned at the stake. Previously, there had been four decades of continuous warfare. The peace he brought lasted for almost 25 years. "Peace flourisheth in Sweden, because Herr Sten ruleth." is inscribed in Latin on a church door outside of Uppsala. During Sten's reign

Wood sculpture of Saint George and the Dragon representing
King Christian I
Source: The National Swedish Art Museums
Swedish Portrait Archives

Scandinavia established its first university, which was opened at Uppsala in 1477. The first book printed in Sweden was by a German immigrant in 1483 during Sten's reign.

Sten Sture was very popular with the common man. He would visit their homes. He knew how to put up a great front for the public. In private life he could be a ruthless, unscrupulous businessman and land speculator who collected other men's estates. When his Uncle Karl Knutsson Bonde died, he acquired property by withholding it from the rightful legatees. He speculated in land, mills and waterfalls, and his methods of acquiring them were often considered illegal. By modern definition, he would have been considered a robber baron and real estate shark. He would buy up land and sell it off at 200 percent profit. Yet even with his faults, he was considered one of the most remarkable personalities in Sweden during the 15th century.

Sten Sture the Elder stayed in power for over 27 years. Finally, even though he had always ruled as regent, jealousy of the nobles and bishops forced him to recognize Christian I's son, Hans, as the successor and king of Sweden. Hans was also known as John I of Denmark. When Hans ruled Sweden, he once saw a five year old boy in the hall at Stockholm castle. The young fellow appeared to him as a born leader and King Hans patted him on the head and said, "You will be a great man in your day if you live." When Hans found out that the boy was the great nephew of Sten Sture the Elder, he wanted to take him to Denmark. Sten Sture immediately had the boy moved from the presence of the king. This young fellow was Gustavus Ericsson, later to be called Gustavus Vasa, who was to launch Sweden on her path to greatness. King Hans, with Sten Sture remaining as regent, never firmly established himself as king of Sweden. Within a year of first spotting the child, he had to flee Sweden. He had served as the Swedish king for only four years.

Hans left his queen, Kristina, in charge of 1,000 men to defend Stockholm castle. Only 70 were left when the castle fell into the hands of the Sture party nine months later. Kristina was taken prisoner. Sten Sture personally accompanied her on the journey to the Danish border. On the way back, he fell ill and died. Poison was suspected, with the Danish Queen's physician as the prime suspect. Sten Sture the Elder was approximately age 63 when he died on December 13, 1503.

Hemming Gadh, who had been a faithful friend and advisor to Herr Sture, was a tremendous influence in the Middle Ages. He served as an important advisor to all three Stures and represented them as ambassador to Rome. Anti-Danish, he was at one time imprisoned in Denmark.

Dr Gadh, accompanying the party, acted quickly when he learned of Sten Sture's death. Time was needed for the Sture party to consolidate its power. Knowledge of Sten's death was kept from the Danish King. Hemming Gadh obtained a strict oath of secrecy from all in the regent's party, who knew of his death. Sten's corpse was covered with skins, hidden on a ledge and left to the elements in the middle of the winter. Lasse Birgersson, a longtime faithful servant who somewhat resembled Sten Sture, was instructed by Dr Hemming don the dead man's clothes and rings and he was placed on Sten's well-known horse. For fear that he

might be recognized at some stop, Lasse Birgersson
eyes were blindfolded under the pretext that Sten had
some eye trouble and could not recognize some people.
Hemming Gadh did all of the talking, claiming that
during Sten Sture's temporary illness, he had given
Gadh plenary powers. Dr Gadh sent word ahead to
Svante Nilsson, a relative of Sten's in Stockholm, that
Sweden would need a new regent. An assembly of
nobles was called, but the real reason for their meeting
and the old regent's death were not revealed until after
the party's arrival.

Svante Nilsson
(Regent 1503-1512)

Once elected, Herr Svante Nilsson immediately
consolidated his power by occupying Stockholm Castle
and other fortresses. Svante, second of the Stures to
rule, was of another branch of the Sture family. His
political coup had been engineered by Dr Hemming
Gadh, whose lessons of two years in Rome had not
been lost.

Not much has been written about Svante Nilsson, as he
was not so colorful as Sten Sture the Elder or his own
son, Sten Sture the Younger. Svante was the first
Swedish ruler to call on German mercenaries. King
Albert III had used the Germans, but was, himself, a
German. During the latter part of the reign of Sten
Sture the Elder, there had been continuous warfare
with the Danes. At times it looked as though the
Swedes could lose. The Danes had joined forces with
the Hanseatic League and blockaded Swedish harbors,

which prevented the importation of salt. This commodity was the very life blood of Sweden. The peasants used it to preserve meat, butter and fish.

The people became tired of war. In some provinces they even refused to bear arms. When Svante Nilsson could not raise troops in Sweden, he recruited German cavalry and infantry. Due to abuse from these foreigners, the professional German soldiers became hated by the Swedish population. When the Germans were not paid on time, they plundered Swedish villages. Since Denmark also employed Germans, there were times when Germans killed Germans on Swedish soil. Kalmar, held by the Danes, was considered one of the strongest castles in Sweden. The Swedes had unsuccessfully besieged it for six years from 1503 to 1509. It was the 60 year old bishop, Dr Hemming Gadh, serving under Svante Nilsson, who led the final siege that won Kalmar. Hemming Gadh was actually more adept at war than affairs of religion.

The regency of Svante Nilsson lasted nine years from 1503 to 1512. His life ended as unexpectedly as Sten Sture the Elder's. Svante had attended an assembly in the District of Bergslange, where a rich silver mine had been discovered. He died from what was presumed to be a stroke while at the meeting. Again, his death was kept secret, so preparations could be made for the election of his son, who became known as Sten Sture the Younger.

Sten Sture the Younger
(Regent 1512-1520)
(1493?-1520)

When Svante died, political power was still seesawing between King Hans of Denmark and the Swedish party. Sten Sture the Younger seized leadership of the Swedish party. The greatest opponent of this third Sture was Archbishop Eric Trolle of Uppsala.

Contemporaries of Sten Sture the Younger included young Charles of Spain who visited Sweden and later became Emperor Charles V. It was the time of Catherine of Aragon and her husband, Henry VIII of England. Martin Luther was having his conflicts with the Pope in Rome.

Sten Sture the Younger was a more interesting person than his father, and many claim him to be one of Sweden's greatest heros. He became a knight at the age of four. When a peace treaty was made between the Swedes and the Union monarch, his father, Svante, had helped make Hans, the Danish monarch, king of Sweden. One of the factors of the peace agreement was that a certain number of Swedes would be knighted. This knighting of a four old irritated some of the nobles, but it was a good laugh for the commoners. They sang ditties which implied that aristocratic females pled that they should also be knighted as they carried future knights in their bellies.

Sten Sture the Younger was 20 years old when he came to power. He had already married 17 year old Christina Gyllenstierna. His father, Svante Nilsson,

had not used the Sture name, but the Younger
recognized the value that the name carried with the
commoners. so the young Sture immediately assumed
that name. Without hesitating, he took control of the
castles and fortresses that had been commanded by his
father's bailiffs. Then, he politicked around the realm
to gain support for his election as the new regent. He
attended church assemblies, went to the market places
and wherever he could find commoners assembled. He
played on the fear of the Dane and any traitors who
might be among members of the Council of State and
the nobility. Both the nobility and Council of State
were against young Sture, but since he already had
Sweden's fortresses in his hand and the commoners on

Sten Sture the Younger and his wife Christina Gyllenstierna
Source: The National Swedish Art Museums
Swedish Portrait Archives

his side, he was too strong for them. He was accepted by the Council as regent in July of 1512.

Conflict with the Catholic Church was not long in coming. Archbishop Gustav Trolle's residence was destroyed and both he and his servants were mistreated. Because of this attack against Rome's Swedish representative, Sten Sture the Younger was banished from the church. The archbishop with the aid of the Danish king, Christian II, who was Han's son, managed to get Pope Leo X to excommunicate Sten Sture the Younger.

Sten Sture the Younger had proven himself well qualified in battle, but he received a wound just above the knee in the conflict with the Danes on Lake Malaren. Usually this type of injury was not considered fatal. His wound, perhaps, had not been properly attended to, because blood poisoning developed. Sten Sture gave orders to be carried back to his queen, Christina Gyllenstierna. He was moved by sled across the ice towards home, but his death came almost within sight of his castle and Christina. He was only 27 years old, but during his short reign, he had done much to liberate Sweden from the union with the Danes and the power of the Catholic church.

Christina, with her four children in the castle, fought on to defend Stockholm. The nobles felt that her cause was lost and backed away. The burghers and peasants made a staunch defense, so that the Danish army was unable to take the capital. Her message to the peasants and miners north of Stockholm was to gather an army and attack the Danes at Uppsala. Thirty-thousand

Swedes responded and made their attack on Good Friday. Twenty- thousand of these Swedish volunteers were slaughtered against a Danish loss of only 4,000. On the 27th of May Christian II came with a large fleet. Christina held out through spring and summer before she was betrayed by Hemming Gadh. This staunch ally of the Stures urged the Swedes to give up, which caused many to demand that Christina yield. She consented and on September 7th the keys to the city were turned over to the Danes.

With the death of Sten Sture the Younger and the fall of Christina in 1520, Gustavus Vasa took power of the Swedish party. This man was the young child that had been admired by Christian's father, King Hans. Gustavus Vasa was not to rule for three more years, because the Danish king knew how to gain the favor of the peasantry. Many hundreds of Smaland homesteads in 1520 were given a bushel of grain and in some cases a gallon of salt.

Christian II (Christen)
(King 1520-1523)
(1481-1559)

Christian II took possession of Stockholm Castle in 1520 from Christina, appointed officers who were to rule Sweden and then sailed away. At this time Stockholm was a small town with a length of no more than a quarter of a mile. Within the walled area of no more than 25 acres lived 5,000 people. Christian II returned a month later on November 4th to have himself crowned king of Sweden. Sten Sture the

Swedes — From Whence They Came

Younger's old enemy, Archbishop Eric Trolle, placed the crown on Christian's head. A herald from Emperor Charles V of Spain, Christian's brother-in-law, presented to him the great collar of the Golden Fleece. King Christian seemed most amicable, but the next day the mood changed. The Stockholm authorities and many Swedish nobles, which included all the coronation guests, were again summoned to the castle at noon Wednesday. The castle gate closed. The king mounted his throne. Trolle, the archbishop previously sacked by Sten Sture the Younger, stepped forward. He presented an indictment to King Christian, which denounced the conspirators by name and demanded the severest penalty on those who had seized and

demolished his castle at Staket in the autumn of 1517. This had been a grave crime against the holy church and himself. The aristocratic members of the Sture party as well as the mayor's council of Stockholm were blamed. Christina Gyllenstierna, the recent widow of Sten Sture,

Christian II was responsible for the Stockholm Bloodbath
Source: The National Swedish Art Museums Swedish Portrait Archives

spoke. She stated that the action against Staket and against Gustav Trolle had been decided by Parliament in Stockholm, and therefore, was a legal undertaking. She then passed the document to the King which confirmed this statement. Bishop Hanbrask of Linkoping stood up and made his apology for the past predations against Archbishop Trolle. He stated that his vote had been forced and thus saved his own life. The others were cross-examined. King Christian II withdrew with his cabinet and left the patriots in the throne room. After darkness, the doors were flung open and Danish soldiers marched in. Arrests were made and a great many of the Swedish nobility and their servants were imprisoned in the Tower, where they spent the night.

On the following day the prisoners were indicted in the ecclesiastical court. Gustav Trolle was one of the judges. The prisoners were declared guilty of heresy, which circumvented the King's earlier promise of general amnesty. Trumpets were blown and the announcement made. Bishop Mattias of Strannas was the first one beheaded. Next, Bishop Bincentius, then three mayors and all of the councilors of Stockholm were beheaded as well as a number of other prominent citizens.

Eighty-two people were slaughtered that day, their bodies thrown into a heap in the market square. Among those executed were Gustavus Vasa's father and brother-in-law. His mother and sister were imprisoned. Sten Sture the Younger's body and that of one of his children were dug up and burned. All properties belonging to the victims were confiscated.

The bodies remained in the market place from Thursday until Saturday. This Stockholm bloodbath roused great indignation in Scandinavia. It took the executioner three hours to complete his bloody task, which meant that there was one every two minutes. Only two days after the bloodbath, the Stockholm burghers, who still had their heads, staged a banquet in the tyrant's honor in the beautifully adorned City Hall. Christian's Queen Elizabeth had given birth to a daughter, so the town gave over to three days of merrymaking.

Christian II, at his peak, was king of Denmark, Norway and Sweden, but he was to be the last Union of Kalmar king. By securing his position in Sweden with the wholesale bloodbath and becoming known as the butcher of Stockholm, he sealed his Swedish doom.

After the slaughter King Christian marched overland towards Denmark, ordering additional executions as he went. Sture's widow, Christina, and her two sons were taken along and thrown into a Danish prison.

Hemming Gadh, who had served the Stures so well before betraying the Younger's widow, was later to be beheaded also.

Christian had been crowned king of Denmark and Norway in 1513 at the age of 32. He had married the sister of Emperor Charles V, the Holy Roman emperor and king of Spain. He was acknowledged by the Council of the Estates and crowned king of Sweden in 1520 at the age of 39. His father, King Hans, had fled Sweden during the regency of Sten Sture the Elder.

Now in 1520 Christian II was the strongest monarch that the Scandinavian countries had ever had. Three years later he was driven into exile. After an attempt to regain his throne, he was thrown into prison, where he spent the next 27 years.

Christian's father, King Hans of Oldenberg, had regarded his son as capable of governing at age 25 and made him governor of Norway. Young Christian , while serving in this capacity, met Dyvke. She was an unusually attractive Norwegian girl, but impoverished. Negotiations were conducted with her mother, Sigbrit, who offered no objections to her daughter becoming the governor's mistress. Christian 's love for her grew and it was reciprocated.

When Christian became king of Denmark and Norway in 1513, on assuming his father's throne, he moved both mother and daughter to Copenhagen with him. They were furnished a dwelling near the castle. Sigbrit Willumsdotter, Dyvke's mother, was a fearless and ambitious woman and her influence with the king grew great. The king recognized that she was a shrewd businesswoman and he gave her many responsibilities over affairs of the realm. This foreign lady had been promoted to a key position in finance and politics. The aristocracy viewed a mere bakeress in this position as scandalous, yet she proved to be one of the best finance ministers that Denmark was ever to have.

 The Danish nobility was hostile to Dyvke because of her humble origin. After Christian's marriage to Elizabeth, her brother, Emperor Charles V, demanded that Christian send his concubine away, but Christian II refused.

Dyvke died suddenly in 1517. The official cause of her death was reported as appendicitis, but poison was suspected. A powerful nobleman, Torben Oxe, had sent Dyvke a basket of summer cherries. They were believed to have been poisoned. Christian, wild with grief and rage, summoned Torben Oxe before the Council of State, but the Council ruled for acquittal because of lack of evidence. The King rejected this verdict and called for another trial. This time the court consisted of peasants, who under pressure, condemned Oxe to death.

With Dyvke's death, Mother Sigbrit's influence with the king became even stronger. The king was in a psychologcal crisis. All restraint was set aside; passions ruled him. The Stockholm bloodbath, which engendered him the title, Christian the Tyrant, was a manifestation of the royal disposition.

Christian, who had hoped to stabilize his own royal authority by the elimination of potential rivals, had, instead, dealt the death blow to his Swedish rule. The outrage at the slaughter brought the final break between the Union Party and the Swedish Nationalists.

After Christian II was forced to leave Sweden in 1521 by Gustavus Vasa's revolt, he was to rule in his own country only two more years until 1523. During those last years in Denmark, his performance as a social reformer was outstanding. He became a friend of the common people. He created more favorable laws for their benefit than any other ruler of the three kingdoms.

After Christian's fall in Denmark and Norway in 1523, all of his law books were burned at Viborg Assemble as a symbolic ending of his reformist ideas. Christian's objective had been to bring about a social revolution that would have established social equality in Danish society. He wanted to strip away the privileges of the Danish church. He would have set up a national court, whereby bishops and other clerics would be on par with any other citizen. He had abolished laws which permitted peasants to be tied to their estates and encouraged more humane treatment of peasants. All of his reforms ended with his fall.

Christian was driven into exile by his uncle Frederick (Fredrik), King Frederick I, who ruled Denmark from 1523 to 1533. King Frederick reined in the peasants' rights, which satisfied the nobles. Christian's long years of imprisonment at Sonderborg Castle were illegal. There had never been an indictment; he had never been examined or tried, nor was there ever any sentence passed on him. His destiny, though illegal, was not regretted by his Swedish victims; they were all dead.

Gustavus I (Gustavus Vasa)
(King 1523-1560)
(1496-1560)

During the summer of 1520, while King Christian II besieged Gustavus Vasa's Aunt Christina at Stockholm Castle, Gustavus Vasa (Gustavus I) sought shelter on a farm on the south shore of Lake Malaren. Both his father and brother-in-law had perished in Christian's Stockholm Bloodbath. A peasant brought news that there was a price on his own head and that his mother and sister had been imprisoned. When Gustavus Vasa started what was to prove the most brilliant and successful revolution the world had known, he was only 24 years old. He raised a Swedish army against the Danish oppressor.

Gustavus Vasa, Swedish king who had to put down
five peasant revolts
Source: Swedish Institute

With the knowledge that there was a price on his head, Gustavus Vasa set out for Dalecarlia in November and December of 1520. He was disguised as a peasant and sought refuge at a former schoolmate's home. He was not recognized, but a servant told his master that they were feeding a peasant who wore a gold embroidered shirt. His former schoolmate investigated and Gustavus Vasa admitted his identity and pleaded for shelter. His school friend, fearing for his own life, refused him refuge. Gustavus then sought shelter with another school friend near Ornas. This friend openly welcomed him with enthusiasm and then immediately proceeded to advise the Danish authorities of his whereabouts. Barbro Stigsdotter of Ornas warned Gustavus that her husband had gone to tell the Danish officers of his presence there.

Jacob Jacobsson, the pastor of Svardsjo, helped Gustavus to reach Sven Elfson's house in Isola. The Danish patrol followed, but Sven's wife hid him until the soldiers were gone. Gustavus was then taken by Mats and Per Olfsson to the north part of Leksand woods. From there Sven Elfson escorted Gustavus, concealed in a hay cart, across the frozen lake. They were headed for Gardsjo. When the Danish soldiers caught up with them, they thrust spears into the hay. They did not detect his presence, but Gustavus was wounded and began to bleed profusely. Sven hid him on a little island in the frozen lake and moved away. He cut a horse's foot so that it bled. When the soldiers came back to interrogate him further about blood on the snow, he pointed to his horse's foot, and they left. Sven recovered Gustavus from the island and they proceeded on their way to Gardsjo, where his injuries were attended to by Ingel Hansson. Gustavus then made his way through the meadows on the eastern shore of Lake Siljan to Mora, 25 miles away. This put him at the head of the lake, where he was hidden by Tomt Mats Larsson. Still suspicious, the Danes continued their pursuit. When Marget Larsson saw the soldiers coming, she hid Gustavus in the cellar and covered the trap door with a brewing vat. This was the fourth time that a woman saved the future king's life.

On Christmas Day of 1520 Gustavus appealed to the people of Mora. He stood on an elevated mound overlooking low fields dotted with hamlets and with strong rhetoric condemned the wrongs and insults that the Swedish people had suffered from the Danes. He told of his own afflictions and of the carnage that had taken place in Stockholm. With warnings of the evils to come to his proud highlanders, he beckoned them to join him in a war of liberation. Gustavus was rejected and had to flee from town to town. On skis and almost dead of hunger and with wolves on his trail, Gustavus made his way towards Norway, hoping to find asylum.

On New Year's Eve Lars Olfsson returned home to Mora from the South. He told of King Christian's trip through Sweden, ordering gallows to be constructed in every province and confirming the Stockholm massacre. He told of the king's other oppressive measures, including new taxes. Many Swedish nobles swore that they would die with sword in hand rather than submit to this Danish tyrant. The people of Mora, with insight from one of their own, now saw things in a different light. Lars, an excellent ski runner, volunteered to go after Gustavus. He reached the struggling refugee just this side of the Norwegian border. By the time Lars and Gustavus returned to Mora, a group had already been assembled and more were flocking in each day. By Lent, Gustavus had a small army of 400 men armed not only with picks and axes, but a Swedish determination to be free.

Gustavus and his small peasant army marched on Falun, seized a Danish steward and took possession of royal property. Their conquest included a quantity of clothing and silk material. Banners were made out of the silk; his army grew to 1,500 men. The miners at the large copper mine were impressed. They joined forces and encouraged their friends in the neighboring villages to come along. Sweden's war of liberation was on. The village of Rattvik is still held in high esteem for the part that their forefathers had played in the war for independence.

Gustavus Vasa was born May 12, 1496 on an old farm belonging to his grandmother. His family had sprung from ambitious peasant stock in the county of Uppsala, located about 40 miles north- northwest of Stockholm. At 22 years of age, Gustavus had gone on board a Danish ship as a hostage for the safety of King Christian; Vasa was put in prison at Kalo Castle in Jutland. He escaped a year later and headed back to Sweden by way of Lubeck, arriving near Kalmar on May 31, 1520.

Gustavus Vasa's grandfather had married a sister of Sten Sture the Elder. His father was Erik Johansson Vasa, a knight and councilor of state and lord of

Rydbolholm. Gustavus' father was a crude and violent man. Stockholm court records reflect that on June 1, 1489 Erik Johansson Vasa assualted and killed Peder Arvidsson and had his body dragged off his Rydboholm estate. An inquiry revealed that Peder Arvidsson, a citizen of Stockholm, had gone fishing in the river that ran through Erik Johansson Vasa's forest. This trespass brought Erik's harsh justice, death. There were other charges against Erik Johansson for violence against those who trespassed on his property. For his punishment he had to promise to no longer beat, hammer or treat people as beasts. Also, Erik Johansson, in company of others, had plundered the Frosunda Rectory and raped a servant girl. She was forced to reveal the whereabouts of the Rector's possessions. No one was ever brought to trial for this crime, as Erik Johansson was responsible for the administration of justice in this district.

Gustavus Vasa had enormous energy and capacity for hard work. He had a feel for practical affairs and an overwhelming greed for power. In power he was utterly unscrupulous and ruthless. Gustavus Vasa was elected king in 1523 and brought about the Kalmar Bloodbath when his throne was at risk two

Kalmar Castle which Colonel von Melen refused to surrender to Gustavus Vasa
Source: Swedish Institute

years later in July of 1525. Even as late as 1525, the Danes still occupied parts of his country as Gustavus had been unable to remove them even by force of arms. The Kalmar garrison was occupied by Colonel von Melen in the name of the king of Denmark, which he refused to surrender. Von Melen had received Kalmar County and Uppvidinge as a fief. The Colonel's brother, Henrik, was in charge of Kalmar Castle. He sent the king an apology, but flatly refused to surrender. Gustavus found this most offensive as the Colonel von Melen had previously been employed by him and had even been given a seat in the Swedish Council of State. Even then Gustavus may not have trusted the colonel, but he had needed von Melen's legionaries. Earlier Colonel von Melen had been sent to Gotland by Gustavus to seize the island, but the mission failed. Gustavus had then suspected his loyalty. Von Melen had previously served as a colonel under Christian II in the campaign against the Swedes.

That spring of 1525 King Gustavus Vasa called von Melen to Stockholm and again demanded the Kalmar garrison. Von Melen promised to hand it over and set off for Kalmar. On his arrival at Kalmar, which he regarded as his personal fief, von Melen obtained an oath of fidelity from both the Swedish and German soldiers defending the castle garrison. Von Melen left the castle in the command of Henrik Jute, who had earlier done service as a soldier for Sten Sture. The wily von Melen took his brother back to Germany and joined King Gustavus Vasa's enemies.

At great cost of life and material, Gustavus finally captured Kalmar Castle. The defenders surrendered to him on Saint Margaret's Day, July 20, 1525. To reduce casualties Gustavus negotiated and obtained the castle by promise of freedom of life and limb to the defenders. Because of his bitterness towards von Melen, Gustavus broke his promise of safe-conduct. When Kalmar surrendered, all of the soldiers were seized, held prisoner and the king appointed a court martial over which he presided. All of the soldiers were tried as traitors, even though Von Melen had been their lord, whom they had sworn to serve and it was their duty to do so. Von Melen was the traitor, not his soldiers. The court martial condemned them to death on the rack as traitors. This sentence was later commuted to decapitation. The entire remnant of the garrison, believed to be 60 to 70 men, were beheaded, except two servants. The Kalmar bloodbath did not produce the indignation that Christian's Stockholm Bloodbath had brought, presumably because these were military deaths.

Gustavus Vasa broke the economic power of the Roman Catholic Church in Sweden. He founded the Swedish state church, which was Evangelical Lutheran. Bishop Hans Brask, chief representative of the Roman church, fled into exile and Gustavus confiscated the enormous wealth of the Catholic church in Sweden. It was estimated that over six tons of church silver went into Gustavus Vasa's private treasury. Even the small church parishes were plundered. This outraged the country folk, although they benefited by the elimination of the Catholic Church's military rule. This stopped the trains of church horsemen riding through the country and demanding room and board from the peasantry. The Swedes were further relieved of having to pay money and goods for church support.

Gustavus was a master at setting one class against the other. He played the aristocracy against the commoners, the peasants against the burghers and one province against the other. His dictatorship was complete by 1530. After 1529 Gustavus did not summon a meeting of the Riksdag until 1544. Meetings of the Council of State were a mere formality and were tasked only to approve his decisions. King Gustavus created a law in 1539 that commanded that no prints should be placed in the hands of the common people without prior government approval. This was Sweden's first censorship law. Two hundred years later during the 18th century his successors still applied this rule.

Gustavus Vasa was one Swedish king that knew a great deal about agriculture. Having been raised on a farm, he issued instructions to farmers on proper seasons to plant and harvest. His passel of regulations telling peasants how to farm did not set well. The Swedish peasants had cultivated their farms for centuries and were especially angered when threatened with seizure of their farms. His rules did reduce the number of derelict farms and increased the output of grain, meat and butter per homestead. Gustavus Vasa's interest in agriculture was further reflected by his becoming the country's largest private landowner. He owned over 5,000 homesteads at his death.

Homestead distribution at the start of Gustavus' reign was 3,754 owned by the crown, 14,340 by the church, 13,922 by the nobles and 35,239 owned by the peasants. At the beginning of his reign, the church had almost four times as many homesteads as the crown. Thirty-seven years later in 1560, the nobility had 14,175 and the peasants 33,130, but the state now owned 18,136 homesteads up from 3,754 and the church had none. No other Swedish king has possessed such great wealth.

Around 1550 the notion developed that the crown was the rightful owner of all land. The peasants possessed only the right to till it. Furthermore, this right could be taken away. State ownership of all land was an idea that came from the Italian jurist, Johannes Bassarius. Exposure to this theory probably came to King Gustavus through the Germans. He put this idea into policy and practical use immediately. If the peasant was mismanaging his farm, or had paid no taxes for three years the farm was taken by the crown.

Gustavus Vasa was an ally of the aristocrats, not the commoners as Sten Sture the Younger had been. Sten Sture the Younger never had to combat peasant uprisings, but Gustavus Vasa had five popular revolts to suppress.

Dalarna was the main source of Swedish insurrections. Many of the homesteads were small parcels, owned by peasants. These dalesmen were feared by their enemies because of their homemade weapons. They used crossbows which utilized sharp iron-tipped arrows. These same dalesmen had been most helpful in bringing Gustavus Vasa to power, but by 1525 they were trying to get rid of him. The first insurrection against Gustavus Vasa by the dalesmen was led by two Catholic prelates, Peder Kansler and Masterknut. Both churchmen had been evicted from their land by Gustavus and their intent was now to put the Stures back on the throne. Once Gustavus captured them, both prelates were sent to the block.

Gustavus faced his second uprising from the dalesmen during 1527 to 1528. This time the dalesmen supported a young man known as Daljunker claiming to be the elder son of Sten Sture the Younger.

King Gustavus crushed the Daljunker rebellion in 1528. After the promise of safe-conduct the dalesmen were seized at Tuna Mead and summarily executed. Daljunker was condemned to death, but had fled to Germany. That autumn of 1528, the young man was beheaded in the city marketplace of Rostock in East Germany. Tuna Mead, where the slaughter took place, is located in the southern part of Dalarna. This had been the scene of popular assemblies for centuries. By 1971 this blood-soaked ground was a meadow under plow and a ring of stones marks that immortal place.

Only a year after the Tuna Mead slaughter came the Vastergotland revolt. This rebellion started with the commoners in northwest Smaland and spread to other provinces. The king suppressed this revolt by splintering the rebels into factions.

Two years later in 1531 the Church Bell revolt broke out at Falun in Kopparberget county, which is 130

miles northwest of Stockholm. The parishioners of
Leksand, led by Herr Everet, resisted the crown's
seizure of their church bell. Gustavus Vasa in his
revenge took ten lives as well as the great bell at
Leksand. The parish offered to ransom their bell for
2,000 marks, a value of 200 cows. Gustavus Vasa
agreed to accept this payment and pardoned the
insurgents.

Gustavus Vasa came back to Kopparberget County in
Dalarna two years later charging the dalesmen with
conspiring with King Christian of Denmark for his
overthrow. After an inquisition soldiers rounded the
dalesmen up, took some directly to the block and
others to Stockholm where they were beheaded later.
Two of the king's old friends, whose only crime was
management of provincial affairs, were executed. Herr
Everett beat the block by dying first in prison. The
crime of conspiracy was never proven; it was all a
squabble over a church bell.

On the personal side, Gustavus Vasa was an effective
orator and sought to educate his people. Many ideas
brought out in his royal pronouncements are still in
vogue today, but people have forgotten their
origination.

Gustavus Vasa was not tall, being only five foot seven,
but he was a handsome man and a charmer. He had a
round head that was covered with light yellow hair and
he wore a long beard. Gustavus was the first of his
family to become a Swedish king. To increase his
prestige he desired to marry a real princess, but was
turned down by the house of Denmark and then the

Polish royal family. Regarded as a usurper, he was
eight years on the throne before even a petty German
princess would accept him. Catherine was the daughter
of Magnus, duke of Saxony-Lauenburg. This first
queen died shortly after the birth of their son, Eric.
With his violent temper and savage moods it was
suspected by many that Gustavus Vasa might have
killed his wife, but it was never proven.

His second marriage to Margareta Leijonhufbud was a
happy one, bringing forth five sons and five daughters.
The marriage was politically advantageous as it related
Gustavus to leading families of the Swedish
aristocracy. Margareta died in 1551. A year later
Gustavus married his 16 year old niece, Katarina
Stenbock, who was taken away from her betrothed.
Gustavus Vasa was basically faithful to his wives,
although his sons had mistresses and many illegitmate
offspring.

Even after a bloodstained life, Gustavus was not
remorseful. When his confessor, Masterhans, appeared
at his deathbed for a confession, he was sent away.

Eric XIV
(King 1560-1568)
(1533-1577)

Eric, elder son of Gustavus Vasa, became king at age
27. He ruled eight years before he became mentally
deranged. His ultimate fate was imprisonment and
finally to be poisoned.

In his better days, Eric was a suitor for the hand of
Princess Elizabeth, daughter of Henry VIII of England.
There is a portrait of Elizabeth at Gripsoholm Castle
that was probably sent to Sweden during negotiations
for her hand. Eric also unsuccessfully sought the hand
of Mary, queen of Scotland. This pursuer of royal
princesses, like his father, had to moderate his marital
ambitions. Eric married a corporal's daughter, Karin
Mansdotter. He found her selling nuts in the

Eric XIV sought the hand of Elizabeth,
England's King Henry VIII's daughter, but
settled for a corporal's daughter.
Source: The National Swedish Art Museums
Swedish Portrait Archives

Stockholm marketplace. His marriage to a commoner aggravated the nobles of the realm.

Eric, a stately man, was both handsome and talented, but even early on he was considered a little crazy. He was well versed in many branches of learning, loved the fine arts, could paint, sing, play the lute, write, compose music and was an accomplished linguist. Like his mother, Catherine of Saxe-Lauenburg, Eric had an unfortunate temperament. His suspicious nature verged on insanity. He used spies to find out what was being said about him. He drank heavily, but when sober, suffered anguish and remorsefulness.

King Eric was also an astrologer and believed strongly in the stars. Those fireballs told him that he would be thrust from his throne by a fair-haired man. His brother, John, was fair-haired, so was Nils Sture, grandson of Sten Sture the Younger, as well as most of the men of Sweden. Goran Persson, Eric's secretary, convinced him that Nils Sture and a group of lords had formed a conspiracy against him. The suspected lords and Nils were imprisoned in Uppsala Castle. One day in 1567, brooding on this conspiracy, Eric went into the prison and personally slew the defenseless Nils Sture and ordered the others to be put to death.

The horror of this action caused an uproar. His stars spoke truely. Eric's two half brothers, John and Charles, headed an insurrection. After a few weeks Eric held only Stockholm and when it fell, he abdicated and his fair-haired brother, John, took over his kingship. Persson was put to death by the nobles. Eric's years of imprisonment began in Stockholm from where he was transferred to Abo, Finland and then on to Kastelholm, located in the Aland Islands situated between Finland and Sweden in the Baltic Sea. In 1571 Eric was taken to Gripsholm where he spent two more years before being moved on to Vasteras. He was imprisoned in Vasteras for a year and then taken on to Orbyhus Castle in Uppland. On Febuary 24, 1577 Eric's life suddenly ended, believed by poison.

John III
(King 1568-1592)
(1537-1592)

King John III unsuccessfully attempted to catholicize Sweden
Source: The National Swedish Art Museums
Swedish Portrait Archives

On September 30, 1568 John III became king under the title of John III. This was the exact date of the eighth anniversary of Gustavus Vasa's death. John had been a student of theology and held synods (1574-1575). He became Roman Catholic in 1578 and unsuccessfully attempted to catholicize Sweden. His wife, Catherine Jagello, was the sister of the King of Poland. They bore a son, Sigismund, who was crowned king of Poland in 1587.

Sigismund III
(King 1592-1604)
(1566-1632)

On King John III's death in 1592, his son, Sigismund, a devout Catholic and already king of Poland since 1587, became king of Sweden. Though born in Sweden of a Swedish father, Sigismund was more Polish than Swedish. Under the Articles of Kalmar, before Sigismund could become king of Sweden, he had to swear that he would maintain the Protestant faith in Sweden. He had also promised the Jesuits power. After being crowned Sigismund went back to Poland, leaving his Uncle Charles and a council of six, appointed by himself, to rule Sweden. After a few years of Sigismund's absentee rule Uncle Charles usurped power, took the crown

Sigismund III, Swedish king who was also King of Poland
Source: Swedish Institute

and retained it after doing battle. Sigismund made war against his native land for many years, but never saw Sweden again.

Swedes — From Whence They Came

Charles IX
(King 1604 - 1611)
(Regent 1595 - 1604)

The third son of Gustavus Vasa, Charles , who replaced his nephew, Sigismund, was only 18 when he and his brother, John, rebelled against their half brother, Eric XIV. Under Charles ' regency for Sigismund, Catholicism was suppressed and the Protestant faith restored to Sweden. By 1597 Sweden was virtually in a civil war due to the conflict between Charles and Sigismund's appointed council. Charles wanted to make war on Finland, but the council did not. The Finnish ruler, Klas Flemming, did not recognize Charles ' authority, so Charles wished to bring him down. Sigismund had forbidden the calling of the

Charles IX
Third son of Gustavus Vasa
Source: The National Swedish Art
Museums
Swedish Portrait Archives

Riksdag, which supported Charles . Charles finally took action when the king's appointed council was not sitting. He summoned the Riksdag and quickly persuaded this legislative body to give him the full powers of government. He then set sail for Finland and captured Abo, one of the principal seaports of Finland. This brought Sigismund back to Sweden with an army. They landed at Kalmar in July of 1598. Since the majority of the Swedes considered Sigismund a heretic, they supported Charles . Sigismund was defeated at Stangebro on September 25, 1598 and he fled back to Poland. As the result of this defeat Sigismund promised to recognize the will of the Riksdag, which formally deposed him as king of Sweden in 1599. After Sigismund's brother, Duke John, formally renounced any claim that he might have to the Swedish throne, Charles became king on March 6, 1604. Charles continued his conquest of Finland, where he took cruel vengeance against those who had opposed him. During Charles ' short reign, he was embroiled in war with Poland, Denmark and Russia. Old and worn out, he died on October 30, 1611, leaving his son, Gustavus Adolphus, to carry on the wars. Charles had helped maintain Sweden as a Protestant kingdom and had been the connecting link between his father, the great Gustavas Vasa, and his own yet greater son, Gustavus Adolphus.

Gustavus II
(King 1611-1632)
(1594-1632)

Gustavus II, better known as Gustavus Adolphus, was often called "Lion of the North" and sometimes "Snow King." His grandfather, Gustavus Vasa, founded the Vasa dynasty. Young Gustavus was brought up in the

Lutheran faith. He was well educated, an accomplished linguist who grew up with two mother-tongues, Swedish and German. By age 12, he had mastered Latin, Italian and Dutch. Later, he learned to express himself in Spanish, Russian and Polish. His father gave him early kingship duties. He was introduced to public life at age nine and by age 13 he officially conversed with foreign ministers and received petitions from subjects. At 15 he administered the duchy of Vestmanland and was his father's co-regent at age 16.

Gustavus Adolphus, who launched the Swedish
Empire and was the grandson of Gustavus Vasa
Source: The National Swedish Art Museums
Swedish Portrait Archives

Gustavus Adolphus became king at age 17. With the strong support of his chancellor, Count Oxenstierna, he was declared of age after accession in 1611. Gustavus spent his life at war with Denmark, Poland and Russia. He reorganized Sweden's internal government and brought about co-operation among all classes. He soon had taken back the southern districts of Sweden from Denmark in his 1611-1613 war with them. He defeated Russia after four years of war and made peace at Stolbova in 1617. He fought a long and defensive war (1621-1629) against his cousin, Sigismund of Poland, who again attempted to reclaim the Swedish crown. The victorious Gustavus Adolphus won back Swedish territory and full recognition as king of Sweden.

Gustavus Adolphus, regarded as one of the greatest generals of modern times, is credited with saving Protestantism in Germany and Sweden. The King of Bohemia started the Thirty Years War in 1618. He, a strong Catholic, forbade his Protestant subjects the right to worship as Protestants. They rebelled and the insurrection spread to many other smaller German states, which were then under the Hapsburg emperor, Ferdinand II.

Emperor Ferdinand authorized Wallenstein, a Bohemian noble, to raise an army and put the rebellion down. Many, who sought plunder, flocked to Wallenstein's army. Wallenstein even defeated Christian IV of Denmark, who had come to the aid of the Protestants. Wallenstein's ambition was to build a Baltic fleet and make Ferdinand the emperor of the North. Ferdinand also favored and assisted Sigismund of Poland who was striving to regain his Swedish throne. With a Luthernan upbringing and the conflict with Sigismund, Gustavus was not destined to long remain on the sidelines during the Thirty Years War. Gustavus' battle with Wallenstein at Lutzen in 1632 won the day for the Protestants of Germany, but cost Gustavus his life. He was mortally wounded by a hostile horseman when his group lost their way in a heavy mist on their way to aid the Swedish infantry.

Sweden's century as an imperial power had started with Gustavus Adolphus' capture of Riga in 1621 and had ended with the peace of Nystad in 1721. This peace was negotiated during the reign of Charles XII's sister, Ulrica, and her husband, Prince Frederick of Hesse.

Christina
(Queen 1632 - 1654)
(Under regency 1632 - 1644)
(1626 - 1689)

The astrologers had predicted the birth of an heir, so King Gustavus Adolphus ordered celebrations that were appropriate for a prince in 1626. Christina was born in the Stockholm castle of Three Crowns on December 8th 1626. The king was 32 at the time and had been married six years without an heir until then. Two daughters, previously born, had died a short time after birth.

When born, Christina was first thought to be a boy, the desired prince. Her mother, Maria Eleonora of Brandenburg, took a violent dislike for the child when she learned that it was another girl that she had conceived. Gustavus made no changes in his celebration plans and joyfully welcomed her as a prince. His reaction was, "Let us be grateful to God; I hope this daughter may be as a son to me." He so educated her. When she was age four, Gustavus presented her to the nobles as his heir. Since Gustavus did not trust his wife as queen, he most certainly did not trust her to raise his child. He made his sister, Catherine,

Maria Eleonora, wife of Gustavus Adolphus, who took a distinct dislike to her daughter since she was not a son. Source: The National Swedish Art Museums Swedish Portrait Archives

principal guardian of his heir.

Christina's reign began when Gustavus Adolphus was killed in battle at Lutzen, Germany during the Thirty Years War. At the age of six in 1632 she was king under a regency which ruled Sweden for the next twelve years. The regency of five, headed by the great Chancellor Axel Oxenstierna, was so decreed by Gustavus Adolphus before his death.

Christina had her coronation at age 18 in 1644. She took the oath as king as all of Sweden's female heirs had done on the silver throne. Surrounded by her counselors of state, she promised to maintain the national Lutheran religion. When she assumed full kingship powers, her war-stricken kingdom faced four more years of the Thirty Years War. This was a war that had been going on all of her life.

Her strange ways mystified many. Christina loved horses and was a huntress. She loved learning and spent huge sums on books, yet hired aides from other lands who had very little appreciation of wisdom. She bestowed fortunes on friends, yet lived austerely. She drank only water, slept little and was indifferent to food. Her dress was simple, often using male attire. She allowed her hair to be dressed only once a week, unless there were state occasions to attend. Christina was a poor judge of what was good and what was bad. She wanted lovers, but would not marry them. She said, "I would rather die than be married. I could never allow anyone to treat me as a peasant does his field." In appearance, she was short and plump. Her blue eyes were said to be ice cold.

The great Chancellor Axel Oxenstierna, who served Gustavus Adolpohus and later his daughter Christina
Source: Swedish Institute

This mischievous queen found great fun in making her favorite lady-in-waiting read indecent books to her in the presence of masculine company. She enjoyed having an all girl choir sing devotional chants set to French words of shameless impropriety, without the singers being the least suspicious. She delighted in conversations with philosophers and even brought poor old Descartes to Sweden to die.

When Christina became seriously ill in 1651, she was becharmed by Bourdelot, the apothecary's son. He knew well how to please a neurotic young woman, who was bored with her responsibilities. Bourdelot had spent time in Italy and learned to sing Italian love songs. Christina could already swear like a soldier, but Bourdelot taught her new oaths. He encouraged her in notorious vices. After Bourdelot left the court, there was a succession of envoys who did not add to her queenly virtues. When criticized by her ministers, she threatened to abdicate.

Christina was a strange girl
Source: The National
Swedish Art Museums
Swedish Portrait Gallery

Whitelocke, the ambassador from Cromwell, gave a descriptive account of her in his book, *A Wayfarer In Sweden*. He wrote of his conversation with her concerning her plans for abdication. When asked whether she could forsake her people who loved her, her answer was, "It is my love to the people which causeth me to think of providing a better governor for them than a poor woman can be; and it is somewhat love of myself to please my own fancy by private retirement." He advised her to look well to the revenues should she thus retire. In preparation for retirement she had wagon-loads of treasures taken out of the country. This secret activity went on for a longtime. Few people realized the extent of it until too late. She had taken her priceless library

Queen Christina
Source: Swedish Institute

and palace furnishings. She took the finest gold and silver pieces, most of which were the properties of the crown.

On the meeting day with the senate the great chancellor, Axel Oxenstierna, could not bring himself to make the announcement of her abdication. He had sworn to Gustavus AdolphusAdolphus that he would keep the crown on her head, so he was not the one to remove it. Christina then made an impromptu announcement. Numerous appeals to change her mind were of no avail. She named as her successor, Charles Gustavus, who was the cousin that she had refused to marry.

On June 6th she renounced the throne forever to herself and to her posterity. When it came time for Per Brahe

Queen Christina's abdication in Uppsala Castle 1654
Source: The National Swedish Art Museums
Swedish Portrait Gallery

to remove the crown from her head, he would not do it. She took the crown off with her own hands and handed it along with the rest of the insignia to the marshals of the realm. That afternoon in the cathedral Charles was crowned king of Sweden and while the coronation ceremony was still going on, Christina stole away from Uppsala, never to return to Sweden.

Christina became a guest of the Vatican before taking up residence in Farnese Palace. Over the years, with a natural inclination towards dissipation, her stolen fortune disappeared. Obscurity and poverty found her. She died in Rome in 1689 at the age of 63, forgotten and neglected, and was buried in St Peters. This was a sad end for the heir of Gustavus Adolphus Adolphus, Sweden's greatest king.

Charles X (Karl), Christina's cousin, who became king upon her abdication
Source: The National Swedish Art Museums Swedish Portrait Gallery

Charles X
(King 1654 - 1660)
(1622 - 1660)

Charles Gustavus, Christina's cousin, became the first member of the Palatine family to rule Sweden.

He was the son of John Casimir who was Count Palatine. His mother was Catherine, daughter of Charles IX and sister to Gustavus Adolphus.

Charles X had fought in the Thirty Years war from 1642 to 1648. After becoming king he invaded Poland in 1655 and won the great battle of Warsaw in 1656. The next year he waged war against Denmark. Charles led his army across the ice and won back much of the land of Southern Sweden (Scania). This war was settled by the Treaty of Roskilde in 1658.

Charles XI (Karl), poorly educated under Regency, but he and his queen became master builders of Sweden
Source: The National Swedish Art Museums Swedish Portrait Gallery

In January of 1660 at the meeting of the Riksdag, Charles pressed for more funding for his wars. The King looked ill, but he campaigned in the council for his objective with the same vigor as in war. Suddenly on the night of February 12-13, at the age of only 38, Charles died.

Swedes — From Whence They Came

Charles XI
(King 1660 - 1697)
(Under regency 1660 - 1672)
(1655 - 1697)

Charles XI became king at age five when his father,
Charles X, died. Sweden was to be ruled for the next
12 years by a regency of corrupt aristocrats. Charles XI
assumed control of Sweden at age 17 in 1672. The
young king's education had been sorely neglected
under the regency. He was ignorant, almost to the
extent of being illiterate. He lacked even the very
basics of statecraft.

Within three years he was engulfed in war and suffered
a defeat at the hands of a coalition of the Holy Roman
Empire, Denmark and the Netherlands (1675 - 1676).
The disaster of this Scandinavian war hardened him
into maturity. From then on he worked diligently to
rearm his nation for the conflict with Denmark.

During the second part of the war from 1676 to 1679
Charles led Sweden to victory in the Battle of Lund,
which was one of the bloodiest in their history when
you consider the number of participants involved. Over
half of those taking part in the battle, or 8,357,
perished of which 3,000 were Swedish. This battle,
though bloody, was the favorable turning point for
Sweden. Charles won excellent terms at the Peace of
Nijmegen (1678-79). In the peace negotiations he was
aided by two able statesmen, Johan Gyllenstierna and
Bengt Gabrielsson Oxensterna. With this settlement
Sweden and Denmark came to a better understanding.
Their bargain was cemented by the marriage of Charles

to Ulrica Eleonora, the sister of Denmark's King Christian V. The parents of Queen Ulrica were King Frederick III of Denmark and Queen Sophia Amelia.

Ulrica Eleonora the Elder — Danish Princess who married Charles XI
Source: The National Swedish Art Museums Swedish Portrait Gallery

Under influence of this Danish princess, now his queen, Charles reorganized Sweden. The estates of the greater nobles reverted to the crown. Every element of Swedish society was recast. Government finance, commerce, judicial procedure, education, church government and even the arts and sciences were affected. Sweden became a powerful absolute monarchy. These changes, brought about during his reign, made Charles XI one of Sweden's greatest kings after Gustavus Vasa and Gustavus Adolphus.

Charles XI and Ulrica became master-builders of Sweden. Sweden was in ruins at the begining of his reign, but they left a sound base for their illustrious son, Charles XII, who gave Peter the Great of Russia many bad years. Charles XI died at age 41 on April 5, 1697.

Charles XII
(King 1697 - 1718)
(1682 - 1718)

Charles XII, who became king at the death of his father, Charles XI, was called both the "Alexander of the North" and the "Madman of the North." Charles received an excellent education under the watchful eyes of his parents. He was on horseback at age four and an excellent horseman by age eight. His father's influence was strong. He hated anything French and cared little for diplomacy. Because the nobles were jealous of the influence of the regents, Charles was declared of age and assumed full kingship at age 15.

An alliance of Poland, Denmark and Russia was Charles XII's adversary in 1699. He invaded Denmark and forced the peace of Travendal in 1700. That same year he attacked Russia and won a major victory at Narva. Two years later he defeated both the Saxons and Poles at Klissow in 1702. He dethroned Augustus II of Saxony, made Stanislas Leszczynnski king in 1704 and forced the Peace of Altranstadt in 1706.

Charles remained in Saxony another year and then invaded Russia a second time in 1707-08. He started with a force of 24,000 horsemen and 20,000 foot soldiers. Charles defeated Peter the Great, but on further attempts to reach Moscow, he suffered disasters. As the Russians slowly retreated, they burned and destroyed everything. The Swedes soon ran out of food and fodder. The winter of 1708 was the most severe of a century. Birds in flight fell dead and wine and spirits froze solid. With his small remaining army, Charles XII laid siege on Poltava in 1709 and was completely defeated by the Russians. Now a fugitive, Charles fled to Turkish territory and persuaded the sultan to make war on Russia. The Turks fought the Russians from 1711 to 1712. When Peter

the Great showed signs of submission, the sultan quickly tired of Charles as a troublesome guest and made him a prisoner.

After 15 more months of imprisonment, he received word that the Swedes were pleading for his return. He escaped and fled back to Sweden in 1714. After an absence of 14 years, Charles

Charles XII, whose main adversary was Peter the Great of Russia
Source: The National Swedish Art Museums
Swedish Portrait Gallery

found his kingdom in a terrible state, but raised another army of 20,000 to keep Russia at bay. Charles then invaded Norway in 1717 and again in 1718. On this second invasion at the siege of Fredriksten, he lost his life. When he looked over a parapet of a most

Ulrick Eleonora the Younger, Charles XII's sister who became queen upon his death
Source: The National Swedish Art Museums
Swedish Portrait Gallery

forward trench in front of the fortress, he was shot in the temple. It was believed by some that the bullet came from the gun of a traitor in his own ranks, but this was never proved.

Ulrika Eleonora
(Queen 1718 - 1720)
(1688 - 1741)

Ulrica, Charles XII's elder sister, succeeded him. She served as head of state for only two years and then abdicated in favor of her husband, Prince Frederick of Hesse, who ruled Sweden for the next 30 years as Frederick I.

Frederick I (Fredrik)
(King 1720 - 1751)
(1676 - 1751)

Upon abdication of his wife, Ulrika Eleonora, Frederick of Hesse- Cassel was elected king of

Fredrick I became king when Ulrika Eleonora his wife abdicated
Source: The National Swedish Art Museums Swedish Portrait Gallery G. Lundberg

Sweden. A new constitution divested him of power, so his 30 year reign was dominated by the nobility. There was much strife between the political parties, the Caps and the Hats. Foreign policy was dominated by Count Arvid Horne during 1720 to 1738. During Frederick's reign another war was fought with Russia in Finland between 1741 and 1743.

Gustavus III
(King 1771 - 1792)
(1746 - 1792)

The next Swedish king of some note was Gustavus III, the son of Adolphus Frederick, king of Sweden and Louisa Ulrica of Prussia, a sister of Frederick the Great. Gustavus III came to power at a time of intense party strife and royal power was at a low ebb. He solved his immediate problem by arresting the ruling council as a body in 1772. He waged an unsuccessful war against Russia in 1788 and in spite of this failure he was given new powers by the Diet in 1789.

The elegant Gustavus III became one of Sweden's best orators. He wrote plays, acted in them and gathered about him artists and authors. As an enlightened monarch, he founded the Swedish Academy of Arts, reformed the currency, removed restrictions on trade, abolished torture, allowed religious freedom for foreigners and he encouraged freedom of the press. Of more importance to Americans, Gustavus III was the first non-participant European monarch to recognize the independence of the American colonies.

Gustavus earned the enmity of his people when he prohibited private distilling and reserved liquor making as a government monopoly. He grew more extravagant and his increased absolutism finally turned the nobles

Gustavus III, first non-participant European monarch to recognize independence of American Colonies
Source: The National Swedish Art Museums Swedish Portrait Gallery

against him. At a royal ball he was assassinated, shot in the back by one of his own group, a noble named J.J.Anckarstrom.

Gustavus IV
(King 1792 - 1809)
(1778 - 1837)

At the time of his father's death Gustavus IV was 14 years old. He was born of an unhappy marriage between his father and Sophie Magdalena of Denmark. For the first eight years until 1800 he served as king under the regency of his Uncle Charles, the duke of Sodermanland. Gustavus IV's hatred of Napoleon brought him into a coalition against the Corsican in 1805. This cost him Swedish Pomerania and the last of his German territories. Even with England as an ally, he lost Finland to Russia in 1808.

Gustavus IV's hatred of Napoleon cost him Swedish Pomerania and German Territories
Source: The National Swedish Art Museums Swedish Portrait Gallery

On March 13th of 1809 seven conspirators seized the King from his royal apartments and held him prisoner at Gritsholm Castle. He was compelled to abdicate on March 29th. On June 5th of 1809 his uncle was proclaimed as king under the title of Charles XIII.

Gustavus IV and his family were deported to Germany in December of that year. Later, divorced from his wife and separated from his children, he led a life of poverty for more than 20 years, spent mostly in Switzerland. He died in 1837 at age 59.

Charles XIII
(King 1809 - 1818)
(1748 - 1818)

When Charles assumed his nephew's kingdom, he was the duke of Sodermanland and the younger brother of

Charles XIII made peace with Russia, Denmark and France.
Source: The National Swedish Art Museums Swedish Portrait Gallery
(P. Krafft the younger)

Gustavus III. Serving eight years as his nephew's regent, he replaced him as king in 1809 at the pleasure of the nobles. He had commanded the Swedish fleet in the war with Russia (1788-1790). Charles signed a new constitution in 1809, which restored the limited monarchy. He made peace with Russia,

Denmark and France in 1810. During his reign Sweden and Norway were united and substantial material progress was made for both countries.

Charles XIV
(King 1818 - 1844)
(1763 - 1844)

This Frenchman who became a Swedish king was born Jean Baptiste Jules Bernadotte. He was elected crown prince of Sweden in 1810 and crowned as king of both Norway and Sweden in 1818 under the title of Charles

XIV. His predecessor, Charles XIII, had grown old and ineffective and his natural heir, a grandson, was incompetent. Thus Sweden had called in a Frenchman, a marshal of Napoleon, to rule. Bernadotte had first entered the French army in 1780, where he served in the ranks and fought in the French Revolution. He served in Napoleon's

Charles XIV, a Frenchman who became a Swedish king.
Source: The National Swedish Art Museums Swedish Portrait Gallery
(C.W. Nordgren)

diplomatic service from 1798 to 1799 and Napoleon made him a marshal in 1804 and prince of Pontecorvo a year later.

Bernadotte's wife, Desiree, had been a fiancee of Napoleon. Napoleon's older brother, Joseph Bonaparte, had married Julie Clary of Marseilles in 1794. Julie's pretty younger sister, Desiree, was 18 at the time and Joseph and Julie thought that she would be a excellent choice for Napoleon to wed. Desiree was snippy with Napoleon, the shabby little Corsican who did not seem to have a job, but she did consent to marry him.

Desiree Clary former fiancée of Napoleon, who was to marry Jean Baptiste Bernadotte who became Charles XIV
Source: The Swedish Insitute

Napoleon went on to Paris, where he quickly leaped into fame. Desiree now found him a favored potential husband. During the meantime Napoleon had become attracted to Josephine. Napoleon felt badly about leaving Desiree in the lurch, so had arranged a husband for her, General Duphot. While they were in Rome where the wedding was to take place the general was killed by a shot fired from the papal troops. Desiree actually saw him killed. Then Napoleon brought forth Gene Baptist Bernadotte from Pau. She married him in August of 1798. Napoleon continued to advance Bernadotte all the way up to one of the 18 Marshals of France. From this honored position Bernadotte became the Swedish crown prince.

Unfortunately for Napoleon, Bernadotte proved to be neither grateful nor loyal to him. While crown prince of Sweden, he allied himself with Czar Alexander of Russia in 1812. In 1813 he led an army against Napoleon, which aided the allies in their winning the battle of Leipzig. Bernadotte, who became Charles XIV of Sweden in 1818, was considered ultraconservative. His reign was peaceful and both the kingdoms of Norway and Sweden prospered.

The daughter of Bernadotte and Desiree married Eugene de Beauharnais in 1823. He was Josephine's son. Thus, the reigning family of Sweden descended from the girl that Napoleon jilted and from the woman that he married, Josephine.

After Bernadotte or Charles XIV, his elder son reigned as Oscar I from 1844 until his death in 1859. After Oscar's death, his son, Carl, ruled as Charles XV from 1859 to 1872, to be followed by his brother, Oscar II who ruled from 1872 to 1907. Even today the House of Bernadotte rules Sweden without a drop of Swedish blood.

SWEDISH WARS

Over the centuries Sweden has faced two main
enemies: Russia on the east and Denmark on the south
and west. The wars with Russia were caused by ancient
controversies and Swedish ambitions. With Denmark,
it was mainly to be free of Danish rule. Sweden fought
more wars with Denmark than with any other country.
At least 11 wars took place between the two countries
prior to 1814.

Until the time of the Kalmar Union, there had been a
constant state of war between Denmark and Sweden.
The Union period brought peace for a while, but in the
1430s the conflict began again. Sweden's longest
period of conflict with Denmark came during the rule
of Sten Sture the Elder from 1470 to 1503. The Union
finally broke up in 1814. During its latter decades there
had been continuous warfare. The actual number of
lives lost, if known, would undoubtedly horrify present
generations.

Sweden and Denmark's animosity for each other
continued for almost 400 hundred years and would
erupt into war every few years. Propaganda, generated
by the ruling caste, nourished this hatred, starting
perhaps in the 15th century with the struggles of the
Union. Many of the Swedish songs and ditties
originated while Karl Knutsson Bonde was in power.
Both Denmark and Sweden advertised the evils of
pillage, rape and arson that the other side had
committed, but made no mention of their own
transgressions.

The cruelties on both sides, as witnessed in the Kalmar War of 1611-13, were brought out by the then 17 year old Gustavus Adolphus. He wrote a letter to his cousin, the Duke Johan, on February 13 of 1612, telling about a reprisal raid carried out against Skane. His army had leveled more than 24 parishes of Skane. They had destroyed, burned and killed. There had been no military resistance; their enemy was the civilian population, which included women and children.

It was the battle of Lund, led by 21 year old Charles XI against the Danes on December 4, 1676, that Sweden fought her bloodiest battle, when you consider the number of casualties against the total participants. Sweden won, but lost 3,000 of the 8,357 who perished. This battle cost the lives of more than half of the combatants. With this victory Sweden won back Skane, a land of rich soil created more than 10,000 years ago by the glaciers. Skane became Sweden's granary. From its bounty came sugar beets of such good quality and quantity that sugar was furnished for all of Sweden and an excess left for export. The paternal grandfather of Charles Lindbergh was from Gardlosa, Skane.

The Peace of Nystad, negotiated in 1721, compelled Sweden to cede Livonia, Estonia, Ingria, part of Karelia, the fife of Viborg and the islands of Osel and Dago. This was the end of the great Swedish Empire, which started with Gustavus Adolphus and ended three years after the death of Charles XII, the other great Swedish conqueror.

REBELLIONS

The true heroes of Sweden were not the kings and
queens, whose deeds were usually exaggerated by
history, but those who rebelled against royal tyranny.
Two outstanding rebels, whose lives were lost in
leading major rebellions of the people against royal
oppression, were Engelbrekt who died in 1436 and
Dacke whose death came a 100 years later in 1536.
Chastised and destroyed by the powerful, these rebel
leaders lived on in the hearts and legends of the
Swedish people. The peasant, whose cheek was
chapped by wintry winds and whose back was baked
by the summer sun and whose politics consisted of
only wanting to be left alone, did not forget these
heroes.

Engelbrekt

More statues have been erected in honor of Engelbrekt
than any individual Swedish king. The self-confidence
that he gave the Swedish people changed the Middle
Ages in the north country. Engelbrekt supposedly came
of German extraction. Vastmanland lays claim to him
and asserts that Norberg, a mining district, was his
birthplace. This is substantiated by a court record dated
January 23, 1432. Others say he came from Dalarna of
lower Swedish gentry. His revolt was initiated out of a
compassion for people and to obtain justice for them.
His initial victories forged a will to resist. Engelbrekt's
legend generated more durable accomplishments than
the actual victories that came during the life of his
two-year revolt. His uprising created Swedish

nationalism. Prior to Engelbrekt, the Swedish people tended to think of themselves as Vastmanlanders, Varmlanders or Smalanders, rather than as Swedes.

Impositions against the peasants during Danish King Eric's reign, who was also king of Sweden, caused an almost spontaneous uprising in 1434. The Swedish peasants wanted a restoration of Sweden's ancient laws and customs. King Eric required compulsive labor on his royal estates. Josse Eriksson, one of the king's Danish bailiffs, was headquartered at Vasteras Castle. Eriksson, extremely cruel to the peasants of Dalarna, harnessed their pregnant wives to plows and hay wagons with the result that births were stillborn. Insubordinate peasants were punished by having to sit naked on stones in an icy lake until they died of exposure.

Josse Eriksson's oppressiveness triggered the revolution which started in his district of Dalarna and Vastmanland. By autumn of 1434 Swedish skies were darkened with smoke. Armies of peasants marched through the land and left a trail of ruins. Perhaps 25 bailiffs' castles were burned, most of which were timber forts. Engelbekt's peasants were armed with axes, spiked maces, crossbows and fire. Engelbrekt preferred to settle matters peaceably, but when that failed, force was a weapon he used. His group, marching through the countryside, committed no outrages against noncombatants and did not plunder, as was the policy of royal soldiers. His army of peasant farmers were regarded as liberators by the country folk, who willingly gave them board and lodging.

Swedes — From Whence They Came

Engelbrekt was born with the natural instincts of a military genius. His army at one time numbered as many as a 100,000 men.

Some Swedish nobles fought with Engelbrekt and his peasant army as a means of recovering their own lost power. Well-equipped knights, squires and men at arms joined forces with the peasants and provided much of the leadership.

King Eric finally negotiated with his rebellious Swedish subjects. After several compromises an armistice was concluded.At the next governing council meeting of the Estates of the Realm held at Arboga in 1435, Engelbrekt found himself seated next to Earl Marshal Karl Knutsson Bonde. Engelbrekt was elected captain-general of Sweden, a recognition of actuality. He already was commander in chief of Sweden's military forces. Eric XIII, king of Denmark and Sweden, did not abide by any of his agreements. This was not unusual behavior for rulers at that time. Furthermore, on his way home to Denmark from Stockholm, Eric ravaged the east coast of Sweden, burning as he went.

Early the following year Engelbrekt led a second revolt against this Danish despot. The winter warfare probably cost Engelbrekt his life as most of his time was spent on horseback in adverse weather. Invalided by a rheumatic disorder, Engelbrekt proceeded on crutches to Stockholm to discuss a new agreement with King Eric. Accompanied by his wife and servants, Engelbrekt was carried to the boat for the journey to Stockholm. That evening they stopped for the night at an inlet on an island in Lake Hjalmaren. A boat with several men approached. When Engelbrekt saw Mans Bengtsson among the occupants, he thought them on a friendly mission. Mans was the son of Bengt Stensson, the lawman of Narke and lord of nearby Goksholm Castle. Bengt Stensson had once been an enemy, but they had resolved their differences. Engelbrekt thought that Mans was there to perhaps invite his party to spend the night at his father's castle.

Engelbrekt stood up on his crutches to greet Mans as he jumped ashore and ran up to him. He was expecting an extended hand of friendship. In full view of Engelbrekt's wife and servants, he was struck by Mans' ax. He tried to ward off the blow with one of his crutches, but the ax severed three of his fingers. The

Engelbrekt led first major peasant uprising
Source: The National Swedish Art Museums Swedish Portrait Gallery
(Bentz Nordenberg)

raiding party porcupined his corpse with arrows. Engelbrekt's wife and servants, viewing this in horror, were taken prisoner but later released.

Assassination of such a defenseless person was considered a high crime by the populace and caused a loud outcry. After Engelbrekt's martyrdom he became a popular saint. Miracles were said to have occurred at his tomb in Orebro Church. The lame were cured and illness overcome. Many made pilgrimages to his tomb. Perhaps Engelbrekt's name and reputation came down through the centuries as the result of Bishop Thomas. This bishop of Strangnas wrote "Song of Freedom," which lauded Engelbrekt as a saint and one of God's miracle workers.Bishop Thomas was at first loyal to King Eric, but later joined Engelbrekt's liberation movement.

Engelbrekt's relics disappeared and even his tomb can no longer be seen in Orebro Church. His relics and tomb were probably removed from the church in the 16th century when the Lutheran faith came to Sweden. The Lutherans tried to discourage worship of saints by the peasants. Engelbrekt's murder, believed to have taken place on April 27 of 1437, was greatly grieved by the peasants but greeted with a sigh of relief from the Swedish nobility.

Upon Engelbrekt's death young Earl Marshal Karl Knutsson Bonde became the predominate political force in Sweden. Bonde protected the murderer, Mans Bengtsson, by issuing a decree that none should persecute, denigrate or libel him. "For the sake of peace and quiet in the realm," records concerning this

Swede were destroyed. Mans continued his career as a member of the council of state and later became one of the most respected men in Sweden. When King Kristoffer was crowned in 1441, Mans was made a knight and then in 1451 he succeeded his father as lawman of Narke. The protection of Mans Bengtsson would almost implicate Karl Knutsson Bonde, who stood the greatest gain in Engelbrekt's murder. He was acquitted for lack of evidence. Some believed that the real culprit behind the scenes who caused the murder was King Eric.

Karl Knutsson Bonde, a ruthless man, remained earl marshal until 1448, when he became king. Engelbrekt's right-hand man, Erik Nilsson Puke, attempted to continue the battle that had been led by Engelbrekt. This put him into open conflict with Karl Knutsson Bonde. Puke fell into Knutsson's hands, who betrayed a promise of safe conduct. He had Puke beheaded at Stockholm in February of 1437. Bishop Thomas, who had guaranteed Puke's safe conduct, later bore witness to Knutsson's treachery. Erik Puke, like Engelbrekt, was a man of upright character and a lover of liberty, who had also ended up a tragic figure. Karl Knutsson Bonde, the survivor, wrote the history. In his chronicles he pictured Puke as a scoundrel. The deaths of Engelbrekt and Puke left the peasants without a leader. At the behest of the upper classes laws were passed prohibiting the peasants or countrymen or their servants from bearing crossbow, armor or weapons to church, council, market town or banquet; lest such weapons thus borne be forfeited.

In spite of those precautionary measures, civil violence occurred again when in 1437 the dalesmen of Varmland killed the bailiffs that Karl Knutsson Bonde sent to govern them. During a meeting of the Council of Arbota at Christmas time in 1437, Knutsson declared his intention to march up to Dalarna and chop off the hand and foot of each dalesman. He would then proceed to Varmland and do the same. The fear of being maimed caused the dalesmen to make peace. The malevolence of Knutsson Bonde was akin to that of any other despot of that century. In fact he might have been considered as somewhat humane.

Despite the peace effort by the dalesmen of Varmland, Karl Knutsson Bonde sent cavalry against them. In the winter of 1438 Fryksdal and Alvdal valleys were wasted by Karl Knutsson. Two leading insurgents, Josse Hansson and Torsten Ingelsson, were burned alive. During the period from 1436 to 1470, which was between the death of Engelbrekt and the time that Sten Sture the Elder became regent, Sweden had eight different regimes. There were constant conflicts for power and civil war. At times, there seemed to be no government at all.

The martyrdom of Engelbrekt gave voice to the legends that surrounded his many exploits. To temper the demands of the nobles, Sten Sture the Elder often would employ the threat of another Engelbrekt rising from the ranks of the peasant folk.

Dacke

The Dacke Uprising, coming 100 years after the Engelbrekt led rebellion, was the greatest popular revolt that Sweden had ever experienced. This insurrection was staged against native oppressors while Engelbrekt's uprising had been against the rule of Danish bailiffs imposed by an outside government. Dacke's uprising was a civil war between Swedish noblemen and the commoners.

Nils Dacke came from a family of peasants who owned farms on boths sides of the Smaland-Bleking border, but which were mostly located in Smaland. His family had become reasonably wealthy from exporting cattle across the border. Dacke's fight was to recover those freedoms taken away from the people by Gustavus Vasa.

By the time Nils Dacke led his first attack on a bailiff, he was already a family man with a wife and small son. His wife, Gerstronsdotter, came from the respected clan of Gertons. Dacke was probably about 35 years of age when he came into conflict with the king. Whether he was literate is not known, but in any case, there were educated people around him as he had the support of Catholic priests, who had joined forces with him. The three rectors who gave strong support to Dacke were Thord of Alghult, Karl of Aseda and Rolf of Nobbele.

Dacke was probably one of the most able leaders in Swedish history. He led a full scale war and showed great competence as a field commander. In forest warfare he was on his own ground and the king's aristocrats and German soldiers were at great disadvantage. His guerrilla foresters would ambush the royal bailiffs, down them with arrows and then recede into the dense green background.

Gustavus Vasa punished his rebellious subjects harshly. He condemned peasants who refused to pay taxes or had committed other crimes by having his royal bailiffs put them into dungeons at Kalmar Castle. Close intermarried families were especially harassed. Instead of quelling the revolt, this action only expanded it.

The revolution probably began because of the king's ban on exports. Varend depended heavily on cattle breeding and their export sale to the Danes. When the king declared a penalty of death for selling an oxen across the border, he created a grave obstacle to the economy of the area. The peasants considered this another outrage on top of the king's plundering of the parishes and oppressive taxes. He had robbed the small churches of all of the silver that had come from the toil of the countrymen. After taxation by the crown and the nobles, there was little left for the peasants. Even pigs fed on forest acorns were subjected to the heavy tax of one pig for every five raised. The government even took shirt-linen from poor widows and the dowries of future brides.

Bailiffs demanded their lawful hospitality, free board and lodging in the farm houses. They would also take half a peck of corn and a load of hay. It had become customary to bribe the tax collector above the actual subjected to further outrages when he fell behind on a bailiff bribe-debt. Justice was meted out according to the size of one's purse. Smalander peasants considered the time prior to to Gustavus Vasa's rule, a golden age.

This crown tenant from Flaka, Nils Dacke, led a revolt which lasted over a year and had the majority of the population of Smaland and a large section of Ostergotland solidly behind him. To put down Dacke's revolution Gustavus Vasa required the assistance of all of Sweden's nobility, Danish auxiliaries and over 6,000 soldiers from Germany.

A royal bailiff who had rented land to Dacke deceived him and he lost his land. Unable to support his family as a sharecropper and prohibited from fishing in the river, Dacke lived in the forest as an outlaw. Others in similar straits gathered around him. On June 20, 1542 their group of only 30 men assaulted Voxtorp, a bailiff's farm. This was the beginning of the second great Swedish revolution. Within days he had 1,000 men and two weeks later his group had grown to 3,000 men and prepared for the march on Vaxjo, the main town in Varend.

Gustavus Vasa evoked his defense treaty with King Christian III of Denmark and called upon the Danish king for aid against his own Swedish countrymen. Christian III raided Smaland with 200 men, but was met by 2,500 of Dacke's men. This was only the first of several successful encounters for Dacke 's army during that summer and fall of 1542.

The hard-pressed Swedish king was obliged to negotiate with the peasants, whom he considered to be no better than a pack of thieves. An armistice was made at Linkoping on November 8th and peace was confirmed by Gustavus Vasa's royal brief on November 25, 1542. Dacke's group promised their allegiance to the king and Gustavus promised to send magistrates and bailiffs that were sensible men to Smaland and to rectify other shortcomings. The king accepted this truce only to gain time. Immediately he commanded the nobility to equip for war and called for German mercenary troups to be shipped to Sweden. After completing his preparations Gustavus accused Dacke's peasants of breaking the truce by robbing and burning the estates of the nobles. These accusations were not true.

To further discredit him Gustavus accused Dacke of lying with sisters of the same flesh, namely, with his wife and her niece. Adultery was a crime, so the king's effort was to stir up the people against such a whoremaster. Gustavus Vasa offered Dacke safe conduct to come and negotiate, but Dacke, knowing of the king's past abuse of this code of honor, refused to come.

There was considerable disparity between the king's version of the Dacke uprising and the historic reality. The king described Dacke as having 14,000 men at Jonkoping. Elsewhere, he refers to them as simply a pack of thieves.

Dacke's peasants were mainly illiterate and left no written records. Since the king's party wrote the history of the revolt, Gustavus Vasa's Chronicles painted Dacke as a beast and a monster. He was called a scoundrel, a traitor, a criminal and a murderer. His participants were called forest thieves. As the result of this discrepancy history has usually recorded Dacke as a rebel and reprobate. His support for the Catholic cause did not make him popular with the Lutherans.

At the outset many of Dacke's men operated independently. They would plunder and burn the farms and buildings of the bailiffs and noblemen. They also went after the king's tax collectors. Kalmar County alone had an estimated 727 revenue agents. It was reported in one case that a housewife was making pea soup when called on by the royal bailiff, who claimed the peas as part of his tax. She replied that you shall have them boiled and proceeded to empty her pot of hot pea soup over his head.

Dacke outmaneuvered the king's field commanders. His presence was a strong influence on the fighting morale of his men. The Germans and king's men fought for pay, but Dacke's peasants fought for the right to till their own soil. They wanted the freedom to harvest from the forest, rivers and lakes, a right that had always been theirs. It was reported that Dacke at his peak had as many as 30,000 to 40,000 men under arms. The king's men often inflated the figures to make themselves look good and to explain their defeats. More conservative estimates, which were probably more accurate, put the number at 15,000 to 20,000.

Peasants did not have protective armor such as helmets, shields and breastplates, which the king's men used. The crossbow was their most effective weapon, especially for forest warfare. The Smalanders used crossbows with two foot long, iron tipped arrows. These missiles could be lethal up to 160 yards and could even pierce ordinary armor at 110 yards.

Battle wounds were mostly fatal. To lie alone in the forest, to suffer and die was the fate of many wounded. There was no way to recover them from the woods. There was little medication except for perhaps boiled water. Often wounds were treated with fresh urine, juices or herbs. Barbers extracted bullets and amputated limbs. There was no real anesthesia prior to the middle of the 19th century. Often a blow on the head would provide the anesthesia while the patient's leg or arm was being amputated. Alcohol was also used as anesthetic. Brandy came into use during the time of Charles XII. They would pour brandy down the victim's throat before they started sawing off his limb.

Dacke's final battle was fought on March 20 of 1543 in the area of the present day Virserum, then a small market town. The lakes were frozen and the king's army outflanked the peasants by marching across the ice and taking them at the rear. Four or five hundred Smalanders died in this battle. Dacke, shot by two balls through the thigh, was carried from the field. His loss contributed to the defeat of the peasants. Peasant fought peasant, as the king had recruited other peasant dalesmen to fight for him.

Dacke lived as a fugitive in the forest during the last few months of his life. He went back to the country around Flaka, where he had once tilled a small crown-grant acreage. He met his end in Roddby Forest near his former little sharecropper's farm. He was chased down and shot through with arrows by the king's soldiers. It was believed that friends had betrayed him to buy their own freedom.

The king's men also captured Dacke's ten year old son. According to Gustavus Vasa's Chronicles, the boy died from pestilenzia at Stockholm. At that time there was no known outbreak of plague there. Gustavus Vasa must have found even a ten year old Dacke dangerous. Most likely no one with the name of Dacke would escape the king's vengeance. Dacke's mother, Elin Dacke of Hult, was living on a small farm in Lonbomala from 1551 to 1559. Poplular legend has it that two bailiffs set fire to her cottage and she was burned to death. Olof Dackef Lindo, his uncle, was broken on the wheel, quartered and impaled at Stockholm. Nils Dacke's two brothers-in-law had undergone the same treatment as his Uncle Olof in their own village.

Gustavus Vasa further punished his rebellious people by ravaging their land. Smaland was laid waste and the devastation was so terrible that it took several generations for the province to reach the level of recovery that it had enjoyed prior to the insurrection. This defeat was Smaland's greatest catastrophe. The so called flock of criminals were penned in by a troop of the king's German legionaires. Gallows were erected. Jakob Bagge, in charge, demanded that the people denounce their leaders if they wished to save their own lives. The terrified peasants, standing before the gallows, turned in their leaders and even accused each other. Many innocent people lost their lives, either to the gallows or the block. The soldiers had the king's permission to plunder the rebellious areas. The German legionaires, experienced in punishing rebellious peasants, especially took advantage of it. Before execution, the victims were broken on the wheel and every limb of their body was crushed. All of Dacke's men that could be caught by the German experts perished in this manner.

Burning, plunder, rape and torture were what the people of Varend and More suffered as the king's soldiers passed through. The military enforced a hunger blockade against Smaland, which had already had a bad crop year. Most peasants were fined. They paid with their cattle, which were were driven off to Stockholm. During the year of 1544 after his victory over Smaland, Gustavus Vasa had himself declared an hereditary monarch by the succession pact at Basteras. His Swedish kingdom had been preserved with the help of 6,000 German legionaries, the Danish, and the wasting and destruction of his own countrymen.

The re-evaluation of Dacke was activated in 1927 by a novel written by Ivar Ljungquist, which pictured the conflict as a battle between the small peasant republic of Smaland against a national monarchy. The peasant folk were crushed by the national government headquarter at Stockholm.

Even today the memory of Nils Dacke still has the capacity to generate conflict. The city of Vaxjo in 1955 proposed to raise a monument to him. The city council had allocated the funds, but dissension developed over the project. Conservatives felt that placing a monument to a rebel in front of the governor's residence would be an insult to the king. The city council dropped the matter and it went no further. Shortly afterwards the proposed artist, Karl Milles, died.

Dacke's own province of Virserum erected a statue in 1956. He stands in triumph after 400 years, battle-ax in hand, crossbow on his shoulder near the exact spot where his revolt lay defeated in March of 1543. It was the common man who kept his memory alive. He was their legend. There is now a Dacke Bread, a Dacke Beer, a Dacke Sausage, and a Dacke Football Field. Virserum also boasts a Dacke Hotel and a nearby Dacke ski-jump.

RELIGION IN SWEDEN

Thor, mightiest of the gods ruled over air, thunder and lightening, the rain and weather. On each side of Thor were Odin and Frey. Odin, the god of war, was dressed in armor; he made men bold to face their enemies. Frey with an enormous phallus bestowed peace and sensual pleasure.

Sweden's first exposure to Christianity came from a Frankish monk, Ansgar, sent by Charlemagne's son, Louis the Debonair. Louis commissioned Ansgar about 829 A.D. to convert the wild Norsemen. Ansgar struggled and suffered much hardship, but finally was received by the kindly King Bjorn of Birka. His church was constructed on land donated by the king. Ansgar remained in Bjorn's kingdom until 831, and then left Sweden to become the bishop of Hamborg, a new diocese. Gauzbert, another Frankish bishop, replaced Ansgar at the Birka mission. Reactionary pagans soon drove Gauzbert from Sweden. Twenty years later Ansgar, now an old man, came back as no one else would come. Confronted with the stubborn nature of paganism, Christian missionaries made little progress. They faced many setbacks until the Swedish king, Olaf Skottkonung, from the area of Vastergotland was baptized in 1022. With the death of King Olaf in 1060, almost 200 years after Sweden's first exposure to Ansgar's religion, the Goths (south of Uppland) preferred another Christian king. The Sveas to the North wanted one who would support the religion of Thor, Odin and Frey. This conflict was resolved by an agreement that the Sveas would choose the king, but in order for him to receive the homage of the people in the south, he must maintain their laws and respect their Christian religion.

At the beginning of the Christian period, the Viking nobles lived as territorial lords. The first two centuries of Swedish Christianity were centered around the Gotaland area. Church influence destroyed slavery as an institution and this made large estates less profitable. Small holdings were then leased to free peasants. With the coming of Martin Luther in Germany and Henry VIII in England during the 16th century, Protestantism took hold in Sweden. By 1965 Lutheranism dominated by almost a 95 percent majority.

Prior to the introduction of Christianity the sun was an object of worship in Sweden and the Nordic people still have a strong dedication to it. Early festival celebrations of the Roman Sun God were later transferred to the observance of Christmas honoring the birth of Christ. December 13th initiates the Christmas season. If a family has a young daughter or young relative, they are often treated to coffee in bed with the customary lucia buns, which are called lusskekatter. The young lady is dressed in a white robe with a red sash around her waist. A metal crown of green sprigs of lingonberries with seven lighted candles rests on her head.

Saint Lucia, whom this home celebration honored, lived in Sasyracuse, Sicily about 300 A.D. She developed an interest in Christianity when her mother was miraculously healed of a serious illness. Lucia became involved in charitable works. Her fiance, a wealthy nobleman, insisted that she give up her foolish obsession. She became more deeply involved in giving aid to those in need, even to the extent of giving her wedding gifts away. When his influence failed to change her ways, the nobleman turned her over to the Roman prefect, who placed her in jail. She was tortured and her eyes were gouged out with hot iron spears. Even with this, she refused to relinquish her faith in Christ. Her eyes were miraculously restored to sight and this frightened her adversaries. They condemned her to death by burning, but she escaped out of the fire unharmed. She was finally put to death by a magical sword. Some years later she was declared a saint by the Catholic Church. Her reputation for Christian virtues spread to all Christendom. Dante praised her. The Belgian historian, Sigebert of Gembloux, whose chief work was a chronicle of the years 381-1111 glorified her life in poetry.

When Irish missionaries settled on the western shores of Sweden, they exposed the north country to the life of Saint Lucia as one of Christianity's earliest saints. Saint Lucia was endeared to the Swedes when Varmland was suffering a serious famine. A white-robed maiden, who stood on the bow of a large ship, came to their aid. The lady, encircled by light, commanded that large quantities of food be distributed among the starving people. They had never savored finer food. The Swedes felt that only Saint Lucia could bring such gifts.

The word lucia comes from the Latin *lux,* which means light. Therefore, Saint Lucia is often portrayed in art as carrying a lamp or torch and her head is usually outlined by a luminous halo. Since December 13th is the longest night of the year in Sweden, they celebrate it as the beginning of lighter days. The rugged Vikings celebrated this same day with human sacrifices to the Sun God. Saint Lucia's legend also coincided with an old pagan belief that light was a coveted treasure. The Swedes celebrate the Festival of Light during the Christmas season with the lighting of many candles. Saint Lucia has come to symbolize charity, benevolence and good fortune as well as light. She was treated as the successor to Frega, a Nordic goddess. Christmas is a time when these usually reserved people give expression to their sentiment and joy.

MUSEUM

Around 1870 when folks were discarding old things and going for the new machine-made products, Dr Hazelius was collecting these old cast-offs. Swedish handicrafts and antiques were accumulated. He acquired old buildings that were destined to be demolished. The Northern Museum in Stockholm was founded by Dr Arthur Hazelius to display his treasures. His foresight provides a knowledge of the cultural history of Sweden from the Middle Ages to modern times. His first collections were limited to peasant culture but later were extended to include the more refined society. The Northern Museum houses his Lappland collection. In the war section of the museum is found Gustavus Vasa's helmet, as well as the articles of dress that belonged to Gustavus Adolphus. His apparel, worn when he was killed, had been taken as a trophy and sent to the emperor at Vienna. Later, Austria returned his apparel to Sweden as an expression of their gratitude for Swedish kindness extended to them during the difficult years following World War I. Also in the armory section, there are the few known personal mementos that had belonged to King Charles the XII, including the sword which he used in the Battle of Narva when he was an 18 year old victor. Peter the Great's boat, taken as booty, is also to be found in the Northern Museum.

POETS — WRITERS — ARTISTS

Fredrika Bremer
(1801 - 1865)

Fredrika Bremer is honored by a statue at the Royal Library in Stockholm. She was born in Finland, but in 1805 at the age three her family moved to Stockholm. Fredrika spent much of her 64 years in Sweden. She began to write verses at the early age of eight. She later

became a popular novelist and was published under her own name at a time when most women found it necessary to shelter their writing efforts under cover of a masculine name in order to get published. Her early views, set forth in novels, made her a pioneer in the emancipation of women.

Fredrika Bremer, Swedish writer who was a pioneer in the emancipation of women.
Source: The National Swedish Art Museums Swedish Portrait Gallery (O.J. Sodermark)

Swedes — From Whence They Came

Her influence was great on women's thoughts throughout northern Europe. She was the author of *Sketches of Everyday Life* (1828), a series of romances. She wrote *Hertha* (1856) and *Father and Daughter* (1858), both of which brought out her views on equal rights for women.

Fredrika Bremer made one visit to the United States (1849-51) and wrote an interesting account of that visit in *Hemmen I Den Nya Verlden* consisting of three volumes (1853-54), which was one of Sweden's most interesting travel books.

Esaias Tegner
(1782 - 1846)

Tegner, bishop of Vexio in 1824, was once described by Henry Wadsworth Longfellow as Sweden's greatest poet. Tegner was the leading representative of the Gothic school in Swedish literature. His works include, *War Son for the Militia of Scania* (1808), *Sweden* (1811), *The Children of the Lord's Supper* (1820), *Axel* (1822) and *Frithjofs Saga* (1822).

Johan Tobias Sergel
(1740 - 1814)

Von Sergel, Sweden's greatest sculptor, is also one of her greatest artists regardless of the media. Sergel did the memorial plaque dedicated to Rene Descartes. The French philosopher, who had been the invited guest of Queen Christina, died on February 1, 1650, while on his visit to Stockholm. The Descartes Memorial Plaque

Johan Tobias Sergel is regarded as
Sweden's greatest sculptor.
Source: The National Swedish Art
Museums Swedish Portrait Gallery
(E. Martin)

is located in Stockholm about three blocks north of the Haymarket.

Another prominent work of Sergel's, also found in Stockholm, is a statue of Gustavus the II (Gustavus Adolphus). The monument is located close to the Royal palace on the exact spot where Gustavus first landed in 1790 after his return from the Russian war, which ended Russia's influence in Sweden. Von Sergel did the colossal work, *Muse of History Recording the Deeds of Gustavus Adolphus*. His other works include *Faun, Diomedes Stealing the Palladium* and a number of portrait busts.

Johan Ekman, Simon Gate and Edward Hald
Orrefors Glass

Deep in the forest of Smaland, 26 miles northwest of Kalmar, is the world renowned art glass company located in the town of Orresfor. Johan Ekman from Gothenburg acquired a small glass works there in 1915 that made ink bottles and window glass. He engaged two artists and changed production to art glass. Within ten years the little ink bottle factory became the leader in Swedish industrial art. Orrefors Glass is known and cherished throughout the world.

The two artists, who perfected the process, were Simon Gate and Edward Hald. They initially concentrated their efforts in the artistic field, but finally realized that there was a greater opportunity in the creation of beautiful form, that would serve practical needs and be available for modest purses.

There has been a tremendous renaissance in Swedish arts since 1915. Many who became famous in the fine arts did not hesitate to engage their talents in the decorative arts. For example Percy, the painter, turned out plates, water jugs and fruit dishes that were colored in splendid old Italian faience.

SCIENTISTS AND INVENTORS

John Ericsson
(1803 - 1889)

This Swedish inventor was thought "teched" by his own king, a former marshal of Napoleon. Just before John Ericsson left for England, he told his king, Bernadotte or Charles XIV, that he could build an ironclad ship that would be far more effective in protecting Swedish coastal areas than several fleets. The king said that he was crazy and that Sweden had no room for such fools. This same Swedish "fool" created the ironclad ship that tangled with the Merrimac during the American Civil War, and altered forever naval history.

John Ericsson, Swedish inventor who designed the Monitor whose encounter with the Merrimac changed naval history.
Source: The National Swedish Art Museums Swedish Portrait Gallery

John Ericsson was born in Filipstad, Sweden in the province of Varmland in 1803. His grandfather was the chief engineer of mines in Filipstad. His older brother became father of the Swedish railways. The boys' father did not provide adequately for their welfare. Consequently when the grandfather died, their mother took her two boys to the Cota Canal construction site, where she took in boarders. The boys found jobs to help out.

John, who later spent seven years in the army, achieved recognition for his military maps. When he went to England in 1826 he built a novelty, a locomotive, which was entered into a competition that was won by Stephenson's Rocket. John Ericsson was also the inventor of the steam fire engine and the screw propeller.

In England jealousy and criticism dogged his every move, so John left for America. He was 36 then and he became an American citizen at age 45. On his death at 86, his body was shipped back to Sweden in an ironclad warship. On top of his casket, covered with stars and stripes, was a model of the Monitor. His mausoleum is made of Swedish granite and is topped with a bronze American Eagle with open wings plowing the sky.

Emanuel Swedenborg
(1688 - 1772)

Emanuel Swedenborg, better known in Sweden as a scientist, was considered by most of the outside world to be a mystic. He was one of the earliest advocates of the decimal system. Found among his papers was a drawing for a heavier than air flying machine, whose design would meet approval in modern times. Early on he discerned that various regions of the cerebral cortex controlled corresponding motor regions of the body.

Swedenborg, born in Stockholm, became known as a scientist, philosopher and religious writer. He was made assessor on the Swedish board of mines in 1716,

Emanuel Swedenborg, scientist, philosopher, mystic and religious writer
Source: The National Swedish Art Museums Swedish Portrait Gallery
(P. Krafft)

where he served until 1747. During the siege of Frederikshall in 1718 he distinguished himself with his design of a machine that carried boats overland from Stromstadt to Iddefjord. Queen Ulrika Eleonora knighted him in 1719. Swedenborg went on to publish a great deal of scientific material, but in 1743 he began having visions. He resigned as assessor of mines and devoted the rest of his life to spiritual and psychical research. He wrote *Arcana Coelestia* (1749-56), *Heaven and Hell,* and *The Divine Love and Wisdom.* Among his written works is the interpretation of the Scriptures as the voice of God. Swendenborg never proselytized or founded a religious sect, but his followers, known as Swedenborgians, became a substantial religious society known as New Jerusalem Church. Swendenborg, who died in 1772, is buried in the Uppsala cathedral.

Anders Celsius
(1701-1744)

Anders Celsius, a professor of astronomy at Uppsala, invented the centigrade thermometer, now used throughout the world. He first described the centigrade thermometer in a paper presented to the Swedish Academy of Science in 1742. He was the builder and director of the observatory at Uppsala in 1740. He published in 1733 a collection of his observations and those of others on

Anders Celsius invented the centigrade thermometer
Source: Swedish Institute

the aurora borealis. He participated in the French expedition of 1736 to measure degree of meridian in the polar regions. He was an advocate for the introduction of the Gregorian Calendar. His son, Olaf, became the professor of history at the University of Uppsala in 1747 and the bishop of Lund in 1777.

Jons Jakob Berzelius
(1779 - 1848)

One great German chemist has said, "there is not a department in the whole field of chemistry to whose development Berzelius has not contributed." Berzelli Park in Stockholm is named after this great scientist.

Jons Jakob Berzelius invented a system of denoting chemicals by letters and figures
Source: The National Swedish Art Museums Swedish Portrait Gallery

He is attributed to doing for chemistry what Linnaeus did for botany. Jons Jakob Berzelius invented a simple system of denoting chemicals by letters and figures, which is used today. He advocated that minerals should be classified according to their chemical composition.

This Swedish chemist was graduated from the University of Uppsala in 1802, taught medicine and pharmacy there from 1807 and chemistry from 1815. Using oxygen as a standard, he determined atomic and molecular weights of many different substances. He

Swedes — From Whence They Came

conducted experiments in electrolysis and further developed the dualistic theory which was originated by Lavoisier. Berzelius discovered the elements of selenium, cerium and thorium and was the first to isolate columbium and silicon.

Berzelius was made a baron in 1835 because of his scientific achievements. He was sought by many foreign universities, but he would never leave Sweden. His death came in 1848 at the age of 69.

Carl Von Linnaeus (Linne')
(1707 - 1778)

This Swedish botanist is known as the father of modern systematic botany. He has been ranked as one of the greatest constructive naturalists in history, comparable in importance to Darwin.

Linnaeus was born in Rashult located in the province of Smaland. His father was a Lutheran minister. He was graduated at Lund in 1727 and became an assistant to Dr Olaf Celsius at Uppsala in compilation of *Hierobotanicon*, which was a treatise on the plants of the Bible. He wrote essays on plant sex. He explored Lappland for the Academy of Sciences in 1732 and wrote his scientific results in *Flora Lapponica*, published in 1737. In 1735 he received his M.D. at Harderwijt, Holland. While in Holland he made a study of the plants in the garden of his Dutch merchant patron, George Clifford, and as a result he wrote *Hortus Cliffortianus*. He was the author of *Fundamenta Botanica*(1736), *Bibliotheca*

Botanica(1736), *Critica Botanica*(1737), *Genera Plantarum*(1737), *Classes Plantarum*(1738).

After leaving Holland, Linnaeus traveled to England and France and later returned to Sweden, where he

Carl von Linnaeus, father of modern
systematic botany
Source: The National Swedish Art
Museums Swedish Portrait Gallery
(A. Roslin 1775)

established himself as a physician at Stockholm in 1738. He became professor of medicine at Uppsala in 1741 and of botany in 1742. After a tour of Oland and Gotland in 1742, he published the results of his trip in 1745 as *Olandska Och Gothlandska Resa* in which specific botanical names were first used. His other important publications were *Flora Suecica* and *Fauna Suecica*(1745). *Hortus Upsaliensis*(1748), *Philosophia Botanica*(1750) and *Species Plantarum* were considered the foundation for the modern system of botanical nomenclature. King Gustavus III issued a patent of nobility to Linnaeus.

Alfred Bernhard Nobel
(1833 - 1896)

This son of Sweden, born in Stockholm, amassed a vast fortune from his invention and manufacture of explosives, as well as development of the Baku Oil Fields. His fortune was estimated at more than 30 million Kroner.

Alfred Nobel amassed a fortune from invention and manufacture of explosives — created the Nobel Prizes
Source: Swedish Institute

At the time of his death Nobel bequeathed $9,200,000 to a fund from which accumulated interest is paid each year. Awards, starting in 1901, are made in five equal parts for the most valuable contribution to mankind in the fields of physics, chemistry, physiology or medicine, literature of an idealistic nature and finally the promotion of fraternity of nations through reduction of standing armies and propagation of peace.

Among the distinguished prize winners have been the Curies (1903), Theodore Roosevelt (1906), Rudyard Kipling (1907), Marconi (1909), Albert Einstein (1921), Eugene O'Neil (1936), Pearl Buck (1938), T.S.Eliot (1948), and Winston Churchill (1953). Prizes are distributed each year on the anniversary of Nobel's death which came on December 10th of 1896 at San Remo, Italy.

Alfred Nobel was educated in St Petersburg and the United States where he studied mechanical engineering (1850-1854). He invented dynamite (1866), one of the first smokeless powders, Ballistite, (1888) and over 100 other patented items including nitroglycerin.

Carl Wilhelm Scheele
(1742 - 1786)

At the age of 33 Carl Wilhelm Steele was elected to the Stockholm Academy of Science in 1775. He acquired a small town pharmacy in Koping and in between prescriptions did a vast amount of original research. Of his many scientific discoveries, oxygen was the most important. Most of his experimental work on oxygen was done prior to 1773. His book, "Air and Fire," was not published until 1777. He found that candles burned with much more vigorous flame and mice lived longer when they had more oxygen than just ordinary air. His oxygen studies were independent of Joseph Priestly, the English clergyman credited with discovery of "dephlogisticated air," which is now called oxygen.

Carl Wilhelm Steele is given further credit for the discovery of chlorine, barium and manganese, plus the compounds of ammonia, glycerin, tartaric acid, prussic acid and copper arsenite pigment, which became known as Scheele's green.

Carl Wilhelm Scheele, Swedish scientist
who discovered oxygen
Source Swedish Institute

Other Swedish scientists and inventors

Sarrhenius discovered the theory on which modern electro-chemical science is based.

Aretzius laid the foundation of modern anthropology.

Omontelius introduced new theories into the branches of archaeological science which established a firm basis of construction of the historic chronology of Europe.

J.P.Lundstrom first invented the safety-match.

Carl Gustaf Patrik de Laval (1845-1913) invented the centrifugal cream separator and the first practical steam turbine.

COMMERCE AND INDUSTRY

Bank

The National Bank of Sweden was founded in 1688 during the reign of Charles XI, father of Charles XII. This bank is governed by a board of seven commissioners. The chairman is appointed by the King and the other directors are elected by Parliament.

Copper Mine

Stora Kopparbergs Gruva is the copper mine at Falun, Sweden that has excavated an area larger than the Great Pyramid. Over the past seven centuries it has produced over a half million tons of pure copper from ore containing 60 to 70 percent copper. Copper mines rarely produce ore that exceeds 30 to 40 percent. Eighty percent of the world's copper mines that produced over 60 percent ore have been found in Sweden. There was a young miner killed in 1670 whose body was not recovered until 49 years later. Copper vitriol had kept the body in perfect preservation. It was his sweetheart, then an old woman, who identified him.

Stora Kopparbergs Gruva mine, now nearly exhausted, is owned by a company which started in 1220. In the declining years of copper production, the operation has made use of sulphur ore, the by-products of copper vitriol, and mined some gold and silver. The company also has owned vast resources of timber and iron. Their iron mines at one time produced 11 million tons of iron ore annually.

Cooperatives

Kooperativa Forbundet, a konsum cooperative union, sometimes called KF, was founded in 1899 by a group of young people. After five years they were doing an annual business of $75,000 among their society members and with the general public. The public was permitted to trade with them, but did not share in the annual dividends, which were paid to the members. Wholesalers felt threatened and often boycotted the association. KF received so much opposition from domestic suppliers that in many cases they bought directly from foreign sources. When they bucked the Margarine Trust by manufacturing margarine themselves, they forced the prices down and gained a lot of credibility with the public. Swedes were also complaining about the monopoly of the flour milling industry, which made profits of 23 to 33 percent. KF bought mills and brought the prices down there also. At one time Stockholm alone had over 400 konsum shops. Today in Sweden, the consumer movement and private enterprise exist side by side and both thrive.

Swedish Timber

Half of Sweden in 1937 was still covered by forests of which 24 percent were owned by the government and 76 percent privately. Two thirds of the private timberland belonged to farmers and only a modest 2 to 3 percent to the landed proprietaries.

Sweden's economic base has depended upon the timber industry and its forests. She has been a paper manufacturer since 1573. There has been said to be 10 acres of forest for every inhabitant of Sweden. The program of reforestration has been so systematic that forests actually gained more than three million acres from 1905 to 1937.

SWEDISH LAW

Swedish lawyers and lawmakers have been as reluctant as the English to interfere with the so-called common law. Sweden produced its first great law recodification in 1734 during the reign of Frederick I and his wife Ulrica, sister of Charles XII. The Swedish constitution of 1809 was based on an older order somewhat like the United States Bill of Rights.

RECIPES FROM OLD SWEDEN

Credit for these recipes is given to June Alberg Schultz who preserved them and now passes this collection on from her mother, Hilda E. Dahlquist Alberg, who emigrated from Skane, Sweden to Ellis Island in 1891 with her brother, Carl, and her mother, Bengta. After leaving Ellis Island they made the long train trip west to Bellington, Washington, then known as Whatcom, to join her father, Nels Dahlquist, who had immigrated to the United States in 1886.

(Cup(s) = C.; Tablespoon(s) = Tbsp.; Teaspoon(s) = tsp.; Pound(s) = lb.)

FATTIGMAN

6	egg yolks
1	egg white
6 Tbsp.	white sugar
6 Tbsp.	whip cream (unwhipped)
6	cardamom seed (dry in oven—remove from shell and crush firm)
1 tsp.	brandy
1/2 tsp.	salt
2 C.	flour

Beat eggs until fluffy; add cream, sugar, cardamom and brandy; beat. Add sifted flour and salt. Roll out thin and cut in strips and slit in center; then invert through hole in center and then deep fry.

SANDBAKELSER

2 C.	flour
1 C.	sugar
1 lb.	butter
1 C.	ground almond nuts
1 tsp.	cinnamon
1/2 tsp.	salt
3 C.	fine ground bread crumbs

Mold into small fluted tins; slow oven—325 degrees for 10 minutes. Cool. Remove from tins.

BERLINERKRANSAR

(Rich Cookie)

1 C.	butter
2	eggs yolks
1/2 C.	sugar
2 1/2 C.	flour

Cream all ingredients together and chill dough. Form dough in rings and loop over like bow knot and dip in the unbeaten whites and then in sugar and bake at 325 degrees for 10 minutes. Use colored sugar if you can get it.

PEPPERKAKOR

(Gingersnap)

1 C.	butter
1 C.	sugar
1 C.	molasses
1 C.	buttermilk
1 Tbsp.	vinegar
1 tsp.	soda
1 tsp.	cinnamon
1/2 tsp.	ginger
1 tsp.	cloves
2 1/2 C.	flour

Let dough stand overnight. Roll out thin—place blanched almonds in center of each cookie. Bake at 325 degrees for 12 minutes.

ROSETTES

2	eggs
2 tsp	sugar
1/4 tsp.	salt
1 C.	flour
1 C.	milk
1 tsp.	lemon flavoring

Beat eggs slightly, add sugar, salt and milk, stir in flour gradually and beat until smooth. Bake with iron—370 degrees.

KRUMKAKA

2	eggs (beaten)
1/2 C.	butter
1 C.	milk (scant)
1 C.	sugar
1-1/2 C.	flour

Cream butter and sugar; add eggs, cream and then add flour. Bake on krumkake iron and roll on wooden spoon handle.

VESTGOTA KRINGLORS

2 C.	butter
4 C.	flour
1 C.	thick cream
1 Tbsp.	sugar
1/4 tsp.	soda in water

Mix all together, roll thin; cut out with donut cutter. Beat up white of egg and brush on top and dip in colored sugar. Bake in 350 degree oven until golden brown.

SPRITZ

1/2 lb.	butter
1 C.	sugar
2	eggs
3-1/2 C.	flour
2 tsp	almond flavoring

Put dough through cookie gun. Bake 350 degrees or until golden yellow.

BUTTERLESS, EGGLESS AND MILKLESS CAKE

1 C.	brown sugar firmly packed
1-1/4 C.	water
1/3 C.	shortening
2/3 C.	raisins
1/2 tsp.	nutmeg
2 tsp.	cinnamon
1/2 tsp.	cloves
1 tsp.	salt
2 tsp.	baking powder
2 C.	flour
1 tsp.	soda dissolve in 2 tsp. water

Boil brown sugar, 1-1/4 cup water, shortening, raisins and spices for 3 minutes. Cool. Add salt and dissolved baking soda, gradually add the flour and baking powder which has been sifted together. Beat smooth. Can add maraschino cherries and/or raspberries. Bake in greased and floured 8x8x2 pan at 325 degrees for 50 minutes.

LIMPA

(Rye flat bread)

1	yeast cake
1/4 C.	water
1/2 C.	lard or butter
1 C.	milk
1/4 C.	dark corn syrup
3/4 tsp.	salt
1-1/2 tsp.	anise seed, pounded
3 C.	rye flour
1-1/4 C.	white flour

Melt fat, add milk—cool to lukewarm; add remaining ingredients and half of rye flour, mix well. Add remaining rye flour and gradually work in rest of white flour except for 3/4 cup. Beat well until dough is smooth. Let rise until double in bulk. Work in half of flour; turn dough onto floured board and knead well. Divide in two equal portions; shape into round flat loaves the size of a dinner plate. Cut round role in center. Place on a greased baking sheet. Prick with fork and let rise 45 minutes. Bake in hot oven at 425 degrees for 15 to 20 minutes. Brush with warm water and cover with towel. Makes 2 loaves.

THIN BREAD

4 C.	flour
1/2 C.	shortening (plus 1 Tbsp. butter)
1 tsp.	baking powder
1/2 tsp.	salt
1/2 C.	sugar
1 1/2 C.	diluted can milk

Roll out very thin and pierce with fork. Cut with coffee can or odd shape with knife. Bake on cookie sheet at 325 degrees.

RYE BREAD

(Makes 3—1-1/4 pound loaves)

8 C.	white flour
4 C.	rye flour
3 C.	lukewarm water
2	cakes yeast
1 1/3 Tbsp	salt
4 Tbsp.	shortening
2 Tbsp.	brown sugar or white sugar

Sift and measure flours. Crumble yeast; add salt and lukewarm water to dissolved yeast; add shortening and sugar. Add flour and stir; knead until smooth. Let rise 30 minutes. Mold into loaves and let rise in pans 40 minutes. Bake 450 degrees for 15 minutes; reduce heat to 375 degrees and bake 25 to 35 minutes longer. Put in a little molasses if you like it darker or you can substitue Karo (dark) syrup. The addition of a cup of applesauce in place of sugar makes it more moist.

COFFEE BREAD

(Recipe good for biscuits too)

2	yeast cakes. Soak yeast in 3/4 cup lukewarm milk with a little sugar in it—heat up 1 quart milk (lukewarm)
2	eggs
9 Tbsp.	butter and little salt
2 C.	sugar
6	cardamom seeds

Put crushed cardamom seed in batter, measure butter before melting. Beat butter, sugar, milk, salt and egg. Add enough flour to make a soft batter and let it rise. After rising mix flour in little at a time and work it each time and work well again. Let rise again and then make it into loaves or rings and clip on top with scissors and let rise again. When you put in oven, brush cream over top with pastry brush and dust granulated sugar over the cream. Bake at 375 degrees 25 to 30 minutes. Can add fruit for X-mas bread or Easter bread.

SKORPOR

(Makes 50 rusks)

1	egg
1/2 C.	sugar
1/2 C.	butter, melted
1/4 C.	chopped almonds
1/2 tsp.	almond extract
1-1/4 C.	flour
1 tsp.	baking powder

Beat egg and sugar until white and fluffy. Add melted butter and other ingredients. Mix well. Roll into 2 round strands. Place on buttered cookie sheet. Bake at 350 degrees for 10 minutes. Cut in 1/2" slices — separate and return to slow oven 250 degrees for 8 minutes. Turn off oven — leave in oven to dry.

RUTABAGA CAKES

Wash, peel and cut 3 medium size rutabaga and 3 potatoes. Cook in small amount of water until tender. Mash, add 2 Tbsp. butter, salt and pepper. Makes 12 patties. Flour both sides and fry until golden brown.

HEAD CHEESE

4 lb.	pork roast
2-1/2 lb.	veal shoulder
1-1/2 lb.	lamb
1/4 lb.	fresh side pork
1 tps.	salt*
5	allspice, whole*
5	peppercorns*
2	cloves, whole*

(Note: do not use stew meat as there is too much skin and gristle). Place all meat and spices indicated above* in boiling water. Cover and let simmer for two hours or until meat is tender. Place clean dish towel wrung out in hot water in glass bowl. Cut meat into small pieces and pack in layers in the glass bowl. Add some spices to each layer.** When meat is all packed, tie cloth with string creating a bag. Reheat liquid from boiled meat and dip in bag of meat so that it will be hot again. Place bag back in bowl and put heavy weight on it. Let stand overnight and then place in refrigerator. Cut as used. Makes excellent sandwiches.

*   Add these quantities of spices to water sufficient for boiling.

** Spices to add to layered meat: 2 tsp. salt; 2 tsp. pepper; 1/4 tsp. allspice; 1/4 tsp. cloves.

DUMPLINGS
(Serves 6)

1-1/2 C.	flour
1/2 tsp.	salt
1 Tbsp.	baking powder
3/4 C.	milk
3 Tbsp.	melted fat or salad oil.

Sift together dry ingredients; add milk and fat. Stir just until flour is moistened. This makes a stiff batter. Drop by teaspoons into hot stew or soup; cover lightly and steam for 15 minutes.

MUSTARD SAUCE

1 Tbsp.	butter
2 Tbsp.	prepared mustard
1	egg yolk
2 tsp.	salt
2 tsp.	sugar
5 tsp.	corn starch
1 1/4 C.	cold water (Dissolve corn starch in water before adding to other ingredients)
1 Tbsp.	lemon juice

Mix all ingredients except lemon juice. Cook in double boiler; stir constantly until smooth and thick. Remove from heat and add lemon juice and let cool.

SWEDISH MEAT BALLS

1 lb.   beef

1/3 lb.   pork

Grind together twice.

Add 1 tsp. salt, 1/2 tsp. pepper, 1/2 tsp. allspice, 1 egg, 3 Tbsp. cornstarch and 1-1/2 C. milk or water.

Knead well, add liquid a little at a time as mixture becomes dry. Form into balls and *brown in butter. Add 2 cups water; put on tight cover, simmer 1-1/2 hours until tender. Thicken broth with can milk, flour or cornstarch.

*Roll in fry pan with browning to keep round.

MAGIC MAYONNAISE

2/3 C.   Eagle milk

1/4 C.   vinegar or lemon juice

1/4 C.   salad oil or melted butter

1   egg yolk

1/2 tsp.   salt

1 Dash   cayenne

1 tsp.   dry mustard

Place ingredients in mix bowl. Beat with rotary egg beaters until mixture thickens. If thicker consistency is desired, place in refrigerator to chill before serving. Makes 1-1/4 cups.

PICKLED HERRING

1	salt herring, firm
1/2 C.	white vinegar
1/4 C.	sugar
1	medium onion (sliced)
6	whole allspice, crushed
6	whole peppercorn, crushed
1	bay leaf

Fillet herring and soak overnight in cold water in cool place. Remove small bones and skin. Rinse and drain and cut crosswise into small pieces. Mix all other ingredients and pour over herring in glass jar and let soak overnight in refrigerator.

SWEDISH WAFFLE

Beat 1 egg with 1/4 cup water; add 1/2 cup sugar, 1/2 cup melted butter, 1-1/2 cups flour (sifted) with 1/4 tsp. salt, 1 tsp. baking powder. Fold in 2 cups stiffly beaten whipped cream (1/2 pkg.). When baked, sprinkle with powdered sugar.

FRUIT SALAD DRESSING

Thicken pineapple juice with corn starch; add powdered sugar and vanilla to taste. Cook over low heat until thick. Cool. Mix with mayonnaise.

LAZY HOUSEWIFE PICKLES

1 Gal.	vinegar
1 C.	dry mustard
1 C.	salt
2 C.	sugar

Boil this and pour over cucumbers in an open crock and they will keep.

FRUKT SOPPA

(Fruit Soup)

1 lb.	prunes
1/4 lb.	dried apricots
1 C.	seedless raisins
1 C.	tapioca (large)
1	stick cinnamon
1 C.	sugar
3	apples, chopped
1	lemon (sliced thin)
1	orange (sliced thin)
1/2 C.	maraschino cherries
1/4 tsp.	salt

Soak fruit and tapioca overnight. Cook all ingredients except cherries in raspberry juice and water about 1/2 gallon until fruit is tender, if mixture too thick add more liquid. Now, add cherries. Serve cool or warm.

CLÖGG

1	bottle Swedish aquavit (vodka)
1	bottle dry red wine
10	cardamom seeds
5	whole cloves
3	pieces dried orange peel
4	dried figs
1-1/2	cinnamon stick
1 c.	blanched almonds
1 C.	raisins
1/2 lb.	cube sugar

Pour liquor and wine into kettle. Add remaining ingredients, except sugar cubes. Cover and heat slowly to boiling point. Put sugar in sieve with long handle; dip into hot liquid and moisten. Light sugar and allow to burn; continue dipping sieve into liquid until sugar has melted into glogg. Cover kettle to put out flame; put thru sieve. Cool. Keep in closed bottles. Heat Glogg before serving but do not boil. Serve hot with few raisins and almonds in each glass or cup.

24 HOUR SALAD

2	eggs (beaten)
4 Tbsp.	vinegar
4 Tbsp.	sugar
2 Tbsp.	butter
2 C.	white cherries (halved)
2 C.	maraschino cherries (washed)
2 C.	pineapple juices
2 C.	orange pieces
2 C.	marshmallow pieces
1 C.	whipping cream

Put eggs in double boiler, add vinegar and sugar; beating until thick and smooth over boiling water. Remove from fire, add butter and cool. Fold in whipped cream and fruit. Mold and chill 24 hours. Colored marshmallows looks very nice in salad.

CHANGE BREAD TO CAKE

Slice day old white bread (3/4 inch thick). Remove crusts. Cut into strips 3/4" to 2" long. Spread strips on all sides with eagle brand milk. Cover well. Roll in dry shredded coconut, broken fine. Brown under broiler or low heat or toast on fork over coals.

HAM LOAF

(Serve as luncheon meat)

1 lb.	raw lean pork
1 lb.	ham
1	green pepper
1	onion
1 c.	bread crumbs
1 tsp.	pepper
1 tsp.	salt
1 C.	milk
2	eggs

Grind meat. Mix all ingredients. Put in a wet salt or sugar sack and tie up tight. Put in kettle of boiling water and in this water put 1 cup vinegar. Boil 3 hours. Cool in liquid and serve cold.

PEAR MARMALADE

7 C.	pears
5 C.	sugar
2	oranges (use 3 if small)

Put in food chopper. Boil until clear and thick, then place in jars and seal tightly.

CINNAMON APPLES

| 8 | apples, peeled, leave whole |
| 2 C. | sugar, add to water (enough water to let apples float) |

Put in ten cent cinnamon candy. Let cook until candy dissolves. Put apples in, turn several times and cook until tender but not broken. Lift them on a platter and let syrup cook to jelly and pour over apples. Get good red apples. Serve around pork roast, duck or turkey.

RED AND GREEN GOOSEBERRY CONSERVE

5 C.	gooseberries after ground
1 C.	seeded raisins
1	medium onion
1 C.	brown sugar
2 Tbsp.	salt
2 Tbsp.	ginger
1 tsp.	turmeric
1 Qt.	vinegar

Stem and wash berries, add raisins and dried onion. Put through food chopper and then add dry ingredients. Cover with vinegar and boiling water and cook slowly 45 minutes. Seal tight while hot.

GRAPE JUICE

1 C.   grapes

1/2 C.   sugar

Wash grapes. Put in jar, add sugar and fill jar with boiling water overflowing. Put on cap with bond tight. Process in water bath 30 minutes at simmering temperatures.

RULLPÖLSA

Use flank mutton or venison. Sprinkle salt and pepper. Cover with a layer of slices onions, a layer of fresh pork and beef and strips of mutton or venison. Sew together and put in salt brine for 10 days. Then take it from the brine and boil 3 hours. Makes good meat to slice for sandwiches.

BRINE: Rock salt or table salt boiling water. Test strength by floating an egg in it, that will show when it is strong enough. Be sure brine is cold when meat is put in it.

KRÄM PUDDING

1-1/2 C.   raspberry juice or any berry juice or other left over juices

2-1/2 C.   water

3 Tbsp.   cornstarch

Add Sugar to taste

Cook until thick. Cool. Serve with cream.

SAINT LUCIA BUNS

1C.	milk, scalded
1/3C.	butter
2/3C.	sugar
1	yeast cake
1	egg, beatened
3-1/2 C.	flour, sifted
1	cardamo elm seed, crushed

Add raisins, pinch salt, pinch saffron (if desired) to taste.

Add butter, sugar and salt to the hot milk, which is stirred until dissolved. This is cooled to luke warm and then you add the crumbled yeast cake. Stir in the beaten egg. Flour is stirred in gradually and the cardamon elm seed and raisins are beat in thoroughly. The dough is placed in a greased bowl, covered and let to rise in a warm place until it has doubled in size. Knead on a board covered with flour for two minutes. Then roll out in small portions, which are cut into strips about five inches long and a half inch wide. Two strips are placed in the shape of the letter X and the ends are curled in. More raisins are placed at the center of the bun and one at each curled end. They are placed on the greased baking sheet, covered and let rise for an hour. Then it is brushed with beaten egg and baked at a moderately high temperature of 400 F for 12 minutes. When they are browned evenly, they are taken out. This recipe makes two to two and half dozen buns. Saint Lucia Buns originated as a family celebration in Sweden.

HINTS

1. Keep macaroni or rice from boiling over by adding a tablespoon of butter to water.

2. Use potato flour to thicken—more flavor as well.

3. Lemon peel cooked with cauliflower will keep it white.

4. Slice a piece of raw potato, place in fat when making fattigman and donuts as it will pick up the whatnots in kettle.

5. To shell walnuts so they will stay whole, place nuts in real hot water for about 10 minutes before shelling.

6. Place slice of bread on top of cauliflower or cabbage when boiling. The bread will pick up odor.

7. Use ammonia and lukewarm water to clean rug.

8. Use ammonia mixed with rubbing alcohol and lukewarm water to wash windows—dry with newspaper.

9. To remove stains on polished wood surface caused by hot dishes, cover with a paste of salad oil and salt, let stand several hours and wipe off with soft cloth, rub with furniture polish.

BIBLIOGRAPHY

Printed Works Consulted:

Anderson, Ingvar. *A History of Sweden*. Translated by
Carolyn Hannay. New York: Praeger, 1956.

Grimberg, Carl. *A History of Sweden*. Translated by
C.W. Foss. Rock Island, IL: Augustina Book
Concern, 1935.

Lorenzen, Lily. *Swedish Ways*. New York: Gramercy
Publishing Company, 1986.

Moberg, Vilhelm. *History of the Swedish People*.
Translated by Paul Britten. New York: Pantheon,
1972.

Roberts, Michael, *Sweden's Age of Greatness,
1632—1718*. Edited by Michael Roberts. New
York: St. Martins Press, 1973.

Reference:

Encyclopedia Brittanica, sv "Sweden"

So You Are Going There (DK).

INDEX

Photo by Lubic and Lubic, St. Louis, MO

ABOUT THE AUTHOR

Jack R. Evans, long a student of history and biography, has engaged in mining and movie activities, has co-produced *Christmas Mountain*, a cowboy Christmas film featuring Slim Pickens and Mark Miller, and has been active in publishing as well as writing. In addition to *SWEDES—FROM WHENCE THEY CAME*, he has written histories of the Pike Place Market, Renton, Gig Harbor, Bothell, North Bend—Snoqualmie and *LEVANT F. THOMPSON—Hop King—Banker—Senator*.

Works in progress include histories of Federal Way, Auburn, Ballard, a novel based on more than 20 years experience as a stockbroker and investment banker and a book of essays and philosophy to be called *ROLL ME OVER*. Originally from Wewoka, Oklahoma, Mr. Evans has lived in Seattle since 1960. He is a member of AKCHO(Association of King County Historical Organizations), the Pacific Northwest Historians Guild and Book Publishers Northwest.

To obtain additional copies of this
SWEDES — FROM WHENCE THEY CAME book,
or copies of other histories published by SCW Publications,
contact your local bookstore, and if not available please order as follows:

Name	ISBN#	Qty	Price	Amount
Swedes — From Whence They Came	1-877882-05-4	_____	at $9.95	$ _____
Levant F. Thompson	1-877882-06-2	_____	at $6.95	$ _____
Pike Place Market	1-877882-04-6	_____	at $6.95	$ _____
North Bend-Snoqualmie	1-877882-03-8	_____	at $4.95	$ _____
Renton	1-877882-02-X	_____	at $2.25	$ _____
Gig Harbor	1-877882-0101	_____	at $3.95	$ _____
Bothell	1-877882-00-3	_____	at $3.95	$ _____

Subtotax $ _____

Sales Tax .082 $ _____

Postage and Handling $ __1.00__

Total Enclosed $ _____

Name_____

Street_____

City _____ State _____ Zip _____

Phone_____

NOTE: Retailers, Libraries and Museums.
Books are available through Pacific Pipeline and Pacific
Periodicals or can be ordered directly from publisher:
SCW Publication
1011 Boren Avenue #155
Seattle, Washington 98104
(206) 682-1268